The Competitiveness of the Greek Economy

2004-2008

The Competitiveness of the Greek Economy

2004-2008

By Robert McDonald

ATHENS NEWS

Editor: Djordje Crncevic
Designer: Yannis Smyrnis
Cover Design: Konstantine Georgantas

Series editor: John Psaropoulos

The chapters of this book first appeared in the Athens News, Greece's English language weekly newspaper, in 2007.

ISBN 978-960-89200-5-7

Printed and bound in Athens, Greece by Psylidis Graphics Arts
Pre-Press by Multimedia S.A.

About the author

David Tonge

ROBERT MCDONALD is a freelance writer and broadcaster based in London who has specialised in matters Greek for 40 years. He currently is the contributor of the Economist Intelligence Unit's quarterly *"Country Report: Greece"* and the author of Kerkyra Publication's quarterly *"Business File"*.

He is also the author of several books and monographs on Greece and Cyprus including, among others, *"Pillar & Tinderbox: the Greek Press and the Dictatorship,"* written for Writers and Scholars Education Trust; *"The Problem of Cyprus,"* written for the International Institute of Strategic Studies; and *"Greece in the 1990s, Taking its place in Europe,"* written for the Economist Intelligence Unit. He is an occasional lecturer in the UK and Greece on Greek and Cypriot affairs and an occasional teacher in countries of the Commonwealth on behalf of the Commonwealth Journalists' Association.

Contents

Publisher's preface

Greece's six great challenges

Of the many challenges Greece faces at the beginning of New Democracy's second term in office, six stand out as critical: high social spending combined with public debt; the urgent need for continued education reform; the lack of a strategic foreign policy; global warming and desertification; and a democratic deficit and meritocracy deficit.

Social spending combined with public debt: Greece's pay-as-you-go-system requires current workers to pay for current pensioners. Accumulated reserves in pension funds offer some cushioning, but not enough. Whereas a healthy system should have about three workers to each pensioner, the Social Insurance Foundation (IKA), the country's biggest insurer, declared a ratio of 2.08 four years ago, which is barely viable. The Organisation for Economic Cooperation and Development (OECD) reckons that by mid-century the dependency ratio for Greece will plummet to about 1.7, and the employment ministry's social budget published last month thinks it has already reached 1.72, down from 2.46 in 1990.

The government already spends about 25 billion euros a year – the equivalent of ten percent of GDP – to support the system, and that is predicted to rise to 25 percent by mid-century. To this must be added roughly ten billion euros a year spent servicing the country's debt – nearly the equivalent of all taxes collected from individuals and companies. The opportunity cost of maintaining such a heavily indebted economy is underinvestment in education, research, foreign policy, the environment and worker retraining – offensive rather than defensive tools that could carry the nation forward.

We are a long way from fixing the system. An audit of the pension funds is needed to establish their health. Karamanlis, like the opposition, has adamantly denied even thinking about raising the retirement age or lowering benefits. The employment ministry has signalled, instead, that it will introduce consolidation, offer incentives to retire late and crack down on contribution evasion; but it is highly doubtful whether those measures suffice.

Individual retirement accounts are not vulnerable to the problems of pay-as-you-go because people are better stewards of their own money than other people's. Tony Blair instituted an opt-out clause for Britons wishing to divert social security taxes to private schemes, but here there is absolutely fierce political opposition here to the idea of partial privatisation. Refusing to embrace it, however, deprives the economy of innovation, and therefore the young of opportunity.

Education: New Democracy's great challenge will be to implement its promised revision of article 16 of the constitution to allow non-state universities. At the same time they need to implement their revision of law 1268, which introduced term limits to undergraduates, stayed their influence in the election of rectors and introduced textbook pluralism. And they must strike out on a promised overhaul of secondary education, which moulds the nation.

They also need, by the end of 2008, to have completed the first external assessment of Greece's 23 universities and 16 techincal colleges (*see Paideia, our four-page education supplement in the centrefold*). The assessors' success largely depends on the goodwill of faculty, so another political uprising on the streets of Athens over article 16 would raise the political cost of cooperation and could scuttle assessment.

Education reform is basic, because upon it depend the country's ability to produce people who think critically, are marketable, and can make an informed decision on how to vote. The new minister, Evripidis Stylianidis, will have to win over 28 deputies to pass a constitutional amendment. He may win some of them from Laos, but he needs to win some from Pasok, too. The socialist leadership battle may take until Christmas, offering an opportunity for stealthy coalition-building over the next months. That seems to be the only way for the government to achieve anything in time for a 2010 goal to harmonise higher education across the European Union.

The democratic deficit: Since the major parties are the nurseries of most of the practitioners in our democracy, they must, themselves, be democratic, or they cannot effectively channel public feeling. In fact, parties are closed shops: Parliamentary and local government candidates run under their banner by invitation and are expelled by decree. Party leaderships establish policy, and votes in parliament as a rule break down along party lines. Parties and are also autocratically run: Karamanlis established his authority in 1996 by expelling three deputies who voted their conviction rather than the party line on an opposition bill. There is an alternative model. In the US, the Democratic and Republican party leaderships are administrative. Policy and ideology are shaped by the candidates. Individuals run for a party at will, and define it.

Our feudalistic, top-down system combines with another major democratic compromise – the elision between the executive and the legislature. A government arises through its control of parliament. Most European democracies are parliamentary, combining party leadership with leadership of the government; but Greece lacks a backbencher tradition - the 'internal opposition' - which helps to introduce balance. The result is that parliamentary democracy is self-abnegating, because once established a government is no longer obliged to consult the opposition.

The result is that checks and balances are lacking from party leaderships all the way to the president, who merely rubber stamps legislation. Even his constitutional right to return it once for reconsideration is not, by custom, exercised. The system is designed to ensure workability rather than pluralism, but it makes Greek politics excessively partisan.

Even within this tight institutional frame, there is wiggle room for bipartisanship that New Democracy has not taken advantage of. Pensions provide the perfect opportunity. Social security legislation constitutionally may not be hidden as a rider on an unrelated bill. A high-profile social security bill is therefore inevitable at some point. A repetition of the 2001 attempt to save social security, sunk by union action, is in nobody's interest, because it will merely pass the problem on to another administration. The conservatives could appoint a champion, and invite Pasok to do the same, who would together draft a common set of the more progressive positions in the two parties and present it as a bill. Deputies from both sides could then be invited to vote according to conscience. If 151 MPs from among the combined 254 don't vote for it, that will be a truly democratic rejection, not a partisan one.

The experiment is important because Greece desperately needs precedents of bipartisanship in order to begin to heal the historic rifts between left and right.

Foreign policy: Greece hasn't had a foreign policy to deal with its most intractable problems since New Democracy came to power. We need strategies to bring the Former Yugoslav Republic of Macedonia and Turkey to the negotiating table. Both have chosen to let our differences, respectively over the republic's name and over the Aegean continental shelf and airspace, to fester. That is not in Greece's interest in the long term, because it is the Greek position that will become eroded and the challenges that will become more established.

Athens also needs to adopt a clear position in preparation for renewed efforts next year towards a political settlement on Cyprus. Greek-Cypriots will ultimately decide their fate, but they need to negotiate the outcome rather than wait for a risk-free solution on a plate. Karamanlis' fence sitting three and a half years ago allowed Cypriot President Tassos Papadopoulos to cross his arms at the negotiating table, delivering to Turkey its first diplomatic victory on Cyprus in thirty years.

Global warming and desertification: If current warming trends continue, Greece will face a real threat of desertification. The water table is falling rapidly in many parts of Greece and forests are vulnerable to fire because of dehydration and global warming.

We have enough water to grow crops responsibly, but not enough to overproduce. The Common Agricultural Policy, which has encouraged quantity over quality, is at the beginning of its end. New Democracy has said it wants to re-train farmers in sustainable methods, but hasn't pushed the agenda; nor has it re-oriented them into service professions. Instead, Public Works minister George Souflias is well on his way to recreating the Aral Sea disaster by diverting the Acheloos river for irrigation of cotton farms.

New Democracy is also failing to do all it can to counteract the effects of global warming. A long-term strategy must include the reduction of carbon emissions. On paper Greece is set ot meet its EU commitments to generate a fifth of all power from renewable sources by 2010, but that is mostly thanks to decades-old investments in hydro-power. The Public Power Corporation should no longer be suffered to run Europe's dirtiest and fifth-dirtiest power stations, as ranked by the World Wide Fund for Nature.

The environment has proven New Democracy's blind spot. It is highly doubtful whether they will re-train farmers, stop the Acheloos river diversion or re-design the PPC's business plan around renewables.

Meritocracy, accountability, transparency: Greek society is divided into two separate realities. In the public sector there is appointment for political loyalty, tenure regardless of performance, high benefits, low working hours and inflexibility due to unionisation. The opposite is broadly true of the private sector, which offers better services for less and pays the public sector's bill. To varying extents this is true in every country, but it is true to an egregious extent in Greece, and here the public sector lacks the boon of a marketable training.

As the state loses control of the economy (it has fallen to just below 50 percent by the development ministry's reckoning) this inequality becomes untenable. Societies that reward merit grow stronger because they bring competence up the hierarchy and solve problems sooner rather than later. Having witnessed the failure of the system of overprotection to make them happy, Greeks are ready for more accountability. If meritocracy and accountability advance, and their advance becomes apparent to society, corruption, too, will abate because people will acquire faith in the system.

If New Democracy shows the mettle to tackle the greatest problems, and an openness to bipartisanship, they will stand a chance for re-election based on their courage. If they do not, their days are numbered, because voters are aware that mere management is no longer enough to keep Greece abreast of competition.

John Psaropoulos
Editor
Athens News
September 2007

Introduction

I N 2005, the Athens News published the first edition of *The Competitiveness of the Greek Economy*, which was largely a review of the policies pursued by Panhellenic Socialist Movement (Pasok) governments under the leadership of Costas Simitis.

The New Democracy (ND) administration, which took office in March 2004 under Costas Karamanlis, accomplished little on the competitiveness front during its first year of office. It devoted six months to completion of preparations for the Olympic Games in August and September 2004 and spent another six drafting a policy programme.

The present text, *Competitiveness II*, is designed to assess developments during the succeeding two years.

During the period, the ND government implemented numerous measures designed to promote competitiveness, some more successful than others. Corporation taxes were reduced, investment subsidies increased and legislation drafted to govern public-private-partnerships. These measures all impacted on the private sector and had a positive effect on investment.

On the other hand, measures relating to the public sector were considerably less effective. Legislation to reform DEKOs (public entities and enterprises) was introduced, but its application proved slow as it met resistance from vested interests more focused on position than productivity.

Legislation has been introduced to liberalise energy markets, but the way in which it is being implemented means that it will be 2009 at the earliest before there is any substantive competition with the result that hundreds of millions of euros in investment (much of it foreign direct investment, FDI) is in abeyance pending clarification of the operating regime.

A new National Land Use plan was promised for May 2006, together with special subsidiary plans covering industrial, energy and tourism development. At the time of writing (July and August 2007), sketchy drafts were out for public consultation but were unlikely to come to parliament before national elections. If there is a change of minister or of government, there is no guarantee that the work done to date will continue to stand. Billions of euros for investment in property development remain in the pipeline waiting for the planning tap to open. Development of a Land Registry continues at a ponderous pace.

On balance, the government has accomplished more on the economic front than it is generally given credit for. Its communications are poor and it tends to dwell on disparate details of its policy at the expense of a synthesis that would illustrate how its programmes contribute towards a coherent whole.

Instead, members of the government drone on and on in jargon-heavy recitations about how the government is seeking "to create an economy that is at one and the same time socially just, competitive, transparent and extrovert". The prime minister is perhaps the worst offender in this. It is as though he and his cabinet colleagues feel a need to inoculate the electorate against years of socialist inculcation of public dependency.

Not all ND's policies are coherent; indeed some are contradictory and many ill-coordinated, which is one of the major flaws in the functioning of Greek public life. Each ministry (sometimes even departments within ministries) pursues its own policies without reference to others with the result that separate initiatives can cancel out the benefits of one another, viz the case in which a local municipality on Crete agreed to cede land to private developers for a large integrated leisure resort only to have the ministry of merchant marine announce some days later that it planned to construct a container terminal at the same site.

Despite the prime minister's reiteration of his intention to pursue "mild" reforms with a view to building a consensus for change with the trade union movement, the relationship between government and the trade union confederation, GSEE, remains confrontational and combative rather than accommodating and collaborative.

Comparisons are often made between Greece and Ireland, two of the four eurozone countries (the others being Spain and Portugal) that have received Cohesion Fund aid as well as structural fund transfers under the Community Support Frameworks (CSF) with a view to promoting convergence of their standards of living towards the EU norm.

Since the CSF programme began[1] in 1983, Greece has seen its gross domestic product (GDP) per capita (in purchasing power standards) rise from 73 percent of the average of the EU15 to 79 percent - an increase of six percentage points (pps). Ireland, by comparison, has seen its standard of living growing from 68 percent of the average to 130 percent, an increase ten times greater than that in Greece.

Ireland has created something called Partnership in which the trade

---

[1] *Then known as the Integrated Mediterranean Programmes.*

union movement, employers' associations and government at all levels (from local to national) come together to agree broad outlines of economic and social policy (including constrained wages in exchange for substantial social benefits) with programmes delivered through jointly supported agencies.

Greece retains its antiquated confrontational system of wage-bargaining with delivery of social services continuing to be concentrated in the hands of central government departments which are as much concerned with preserving their 'territory' as they are with providing benefits.

On the rare occasions that the private sector takes it upon itself to try to initiate a social programme, such as job retraining, it is inevitably suborned to become part of the state apparatus by a Soviet-mentality administration, which cannot bear the thought of losing control of any form of public activity.

Author's note

This volume was intended as an assessment of the New Democracy government's contribution to Competitiveness during its first term of office. It was being written with a view to the government seeing out its full term to March 2008, however, three days before completion of the manuscript, Prime Minister Costas Karamanlis called snap elections for September 16, 2007. ND won but with its representation in the 300 seat parliament substantially reduced from 165 to 152. (*1)

In order not to delay publication, no effort has been made to update the text to take account of events since August 20, 2007, which is the cut off date for the information included. There have, however, been a number of developments, which colour the presentation of certain events. These have been noted in the text with an asterisk and a number (see above), which make reference to a brief Annex at the end of the text.

Economic environment

G REECE is the third poorest country in the eurozone (EU13)[2] with a standard of living[3] estimated at four-fifths the EU norm.[4] That said, the country has had since its acceptance on January 1, 2001 the second highest rate of growth[5] averaging 4.2 percent compared to 1.8 percent[6] for the eurozone.

The last Pasok government predicted that the Greek standard of living would achieve par with the rest of Europe by 2010 but its forecast was made at a time when northern European economies were still in the grip of a post 9/11 slump and the Greek economy - fuelled by frenetic investment activity ahead of the Olympic Games - was forging ahead at rates that outstripped those of its eurozone partners by up to four percentage points.

ND, campaigning ahead of the 2004 elections, promised policies that would generate economic growth of 5 percent a year. This would have sustained the push for parity but not accelerated the process as European economies by then were already starting to recover. Still, it might have meant equality somewhere around 2015.

Such growth, however, has not been achieved under conservative stewardship. Polices and legislation promoting growth have been introduced but their implementation has been spasmodic and frequently delayed.

While the average rate of Greek GDP has remained strong (4.2 percent) during ND's term to date, economic recovery in the eurozone has meant that the growth rate of partner countries has increased relatively faster, with the result that the advantageous differential is steadily narrowing.

From four pps in 2003 it contracted to 1.6 pps in 2006 and, on the basis of European Commission projections, will narrow to 1.1 pps this

---

[2] *After Portugal and Slovenia.*

[3] *Measured as gross domestic product per capita in purchasing power standards.*

[4] *Table 9, Statistical Annex of* European Economy, *European Commission, Spring 2007. The European Commission estimate for 2007 is 79.7 percent. The EU norm continues to be calculated as EU15=100; it has not yet been expanded to take account of the enlargement states that entered in 2004 and 2007. The average GDP per cap of the 13 eurozone nations is 97.8 percent that of the EU15, which includes three rich nations - Sweden, Denmark and the UK - that do not adhere to the Economic and Monetary Union. The Greek standard of living is higher, however, than that of all the 2004 and 2007 enlargement states save Cyprus (81.5 percent). Cyprus is to join the eurozone on January 1, 2008.*

[5] *After Ireland.*

[6] *Table 10, Statistical Annex of* European Economy, *Spring 2007. Based on actual figures to 2006 and European Commission forecast for 2007 and 2008.*

year. At such a rate it will more likely be 2025 before the Greek standard of living reaches par with the rest of the eurozone. The ever-pragmatic central bank, the Bank of Greece, has talked of 2030.

Table 1. Real GDP growth, Greece and the eurozone

Year	Greece (percent)	EU12 (percent)	Differential (percentage points)
1971-80	4.6	3.3	1.3
1981-90	0.7	2.5	-1.8
1991-00	2.3	2.2	0.1
2001	5.1	1.9	3.2
2002	3.8	0.9	2.9
2003	4.8	0.8	4.0
2004	4.7	2.0	2.7
2005	3.7	1.4	2.3
2006	4.3	2.7	1.6
2007[a]	3.7	2.6[b]	1.1
2008[a]	3.7	2.5[b]	1.2

[a]European Commission estimates. [b]EU13; Slovenia joined on January 1, 2007. Cyprus will join on January 1, 2008 but calculations have not yet been made for the EU14.

Source: Statistical Annex, *European Economy*, European Commission, Spring 2007.

The high Greek rates of growth are driven by consumption and investment. Private consumption in 2006 accounted for approximately two-thirds of total GDP and government consumption for another 15.8 percent.[8] Gross fixed capital formation contributed 25.6 percent.[9]

The high level of private consumption reflects the fact that Greeks live beyond their (apparent) means. As already has been noted, GDP per capita is just under 80 percent of the eurozone norm; however, private consumption per capita stands at 92.6 percent. Since wages stand at around 75 percent of the EU average, this means the high consumption rate is fuelled by a combination of debt and untaxed wealth from the black economy.

---

[8] *Table 17. Statistical Annex of* European Economy, *Spring 2007.*
[9] *The European Commission estimates that in real terms (constant prices of 2000). Greek investment growth during 2001-2008 will average 6.8 percent a year compared to 2.2 percent in the eurozone. Table 20. Statistical Annex of* European Economy, *Spring 2007.*

Commercial bank credit to households during the years since 2000 has grown at rates of over 25 percent a year (in excess of 30 percent in 2004 and 2005 in the wake of the lifting of Bank of Greece controls on consumer credit). The ratio of private credit to GPD is still the lowest in the euro area[10] but non-performing loans are more than twice the EU average.[11]

A recent International Monetary Fund (IMF) study concluded that Greek banks are more vulnerable at lower credit growth levels than banks in other countries of the euro area because their risk management practices are less sophisticated.[12]

Consumption is further fuelled by unrecorded earnings from the black economy which is estimated variously to be equivalent to between 28.6 percent of GDP[13] and 35 percent.[14] When such funds find their way into the overground economy for the acquisition of goods and services they are captured in growth but also put upward pressure on inflation and promote economic overheating.

The investment component of GDP is driven by private investments, which outstrip public in nominal terms by a factor of six to seven. Some 20-25 percent of private investment finds its way into housing[15] which leaves the household sector with only limited resources left over for savings and investments in equities.

Public investment has been buoyed by EU structural fund aid transfers via the EU's Community Support Frameworks. Under CSF III (2000-2006) there was €22.7bn on offer from Brussels towards a total investment programme of some €50bn which was estimated to have contributed between 0.75 pps and 1 pps a year to the rate of GDP growth.

Under CSF IV (2007-13), now known as the National Strategic Reference Framework (ESPA), there is €20.4bn on offer towards an investment programme of €31.1bn which is expected to add between 0.5 pps and 0.75 pps to annual GDP growth.

---

[10] *84.7 percent of GDP in 2006 - 40.7 percent to enterprises and 44 percent to households - compared with 104 percent in the EU12 - 51 percent to corporations and 53 percent to households.*

[11] *In 2006, 6.3 percent compared with 2.85 percent in the eurozone.*

[12] *"Greece: selected issues". IMF Country Report, No 07/27, January 2007. International Monetary Fund, Washington DC, pp 49-50.*

[13] *World Bank estimate.*

[14] *Informal estimate of Emmanuel Kontopirakis, secretary-general of the National Statistical Service of Greece.*

[15] *Greece has the highest level of home ownership in Europe at over 80 percent.*

The disproportionately high level of consumption[16] and the strong investment growth inevitably sucks in imports. According to Eurostat data, imports in 2006 were equivalent to 30 percent of Greek GDP, while exports were equal to just 20.3 percent.[17]

This means that the negative result on external account dampens GDP growth by between 0.75 pps and 1 pps a year - effectively cancelling out the benefits of the EU structural fund aid.

According to balance of payments data from the Bank of Greece, the 2006 current account deficit soared to €23.6bn, or 12.1 percent of GDP - the highest level in the eurozone.

Prior to the adoption of the euro, such a figure would have been a trigger for a deep devaluation of the Greek currency. But, because the Greek deficit represents only a small fraction of that of the eurozone as a whole, devaluation of the euro is not an issue. It does, however, reflect the basic lack of competitiveness of the Greek economy.

In April 2007, Joaquin Almunia, the European commissioner for monetary and economic affairs, targeted Greece (along with Spain and Portugal) as countries that needed to do more to improve their situation. In a speech to government officials and businessmen in Athens, he said the lack of Greek competitiveness was principally the result of high unit labour costs. According to his figures, nominal wages increased by 6 percent in 2006, while productivity grew by 2.75 percent, producing growth in unit labour costs in excess of 3 percent, a full point above the average in the eurozone.[18]

These higher than average eurozone wage costs in turn impact upon the Greek harmonised index of consumer prices (HICP), the EU measure of inflation. The Greek rate consistently outstrips that of eurozone partners by a percentage point or more. On entry, the differential was 1.4 percentage points. This gradually narrowed to 0.9 pps in 2004 but subsequently the gap has begun to widen to above 1 pps again.

---

[16] *Disproportionate, that is, to earnings.*

[17] *It is no bad thing for an economy to run a big import bill, provided that it is offset by comparable or greater exports. In Ireland in 2006, eg. imports were equivalent to 68.6 percent of GDP but then exports were equivalent to 79.7 percent.*

[18] *Figures produced by the Directorate of Macroeconomic Analysis and Forecasting of the Ministry of Economy and Finance in December 2006 painted an even more mournful picture. They showed compensation of employees to have increased by 8.7 percent in 2006, while gross value added (an indicator of productivity) reached only 2.2 percent, causing unit labour costs to rise by 4.2 percent that year. The forecasts called for them to rise by 3.9 percent this year, 2.8 percent in 2008 and 2.6 percent in 2009.*

Table 2. Unit labour costs, productivity and inflation in Greece and EU13[a]

	2000	2001	2002	2003	2004	2005	2006	Avg
Greece								
Unit labour cost	1.3	0.2	6.0	1.2	4.0	4.1	3.1	2.8
Labour productivity	4.8	5.4	3.7	3.4	1.7	2.3	2.7	3.4
Private consumption deflator[b]	7.6	2.1	2.6	2.8	2.5	2.7	3.4	3.4
Euro area								
Unit labour cost	1.1	2.3	2.4	2.0	0.9	1.0	0.8	1.5
Labour productivity	1.7	0.5	0.4	0.8	1.6	0.9	1.4	1.0
Private consumption deflator[b]	2.6	2.3	1.9	2.1	2.1	2.0	2.0	2.1

[a] *Slovenia became the 13th member of the Economic and Monetary Union (the eurozone) as of January 1, 2007.* [b] *A proxy for inflation.*

Source: Statistical Annex, *European Economy*, European Commission, Spring 2007.

The combination makes Greek exports uncompetitive. An annex to the IMF's 2007 report on Greece[19] calculated that at the time of EMU entry, the Greek exchange[20] rate was probably about right. Since, however, the IMF calculates that the effective exchange rate has appreciated to historically high levels: on the basis of unit labour costs by between 20 and 30 percent and on the basis of inflation by approximately 10 percent.

This means that the Greek goods are uncompetitive unless in some way they are unique. Few are. Most Greek products are manufactured under licence using either foreign designs or processes. Product differentiation is limited. Increasingly, European consumers are looking for quality goods incorporating a high degree of technological sophistication.

An analysis by the Bank of Greece[21] calculated that 49.8 percent of Greek exports during the period 2000-04 were low technology (or resource-based) - the highest proportion in the eurozone - while high-tech products accounted for just 9.4 percent.

The consequence is that Greece is losing market share among its

[19] IMF Country Report, *No 07/27, January 2007.*
[20] *Dr340.75/€.*
[21] Annual Report 2005, *pp 285-291.*

traditional trading partners of which Germany and Italy traditionally were the leaders.

Whereas during the five years 1990-94, 55.3 percent of Greek exports went to the eurozone and just 14.7 percent to developing Europe,[22] by 2000-04 this had shifted to 35.4 percent to the eurozone and 33.3 percent to developing Europe.

Greek exports as a percentage of total imports to the EU15 in 1990-94 averaged 0.4 percent; by 2000-04, this figure had dropped to 0.2 percent.

The problem is compounded by the fact that the relatively high wage regime in Greece means that its prices even for basic products[23] are higher than those offered by developing countries of Asia and Africa with the result that its traditional exports face stiff price competition with consequent erosion of market share even in the new markets.

The Greek government was a strong proponent of EU enlargement not least because it perceived the expansion as facilitating access to new markets. Already, however, there is evidence that buyers in these countries are beginning to look to northern European firms for their imports because of higher quality and sophistication, while looking to third world countries for their basic products because of their cheaper price.

Quite simply, they are looking for better value for money with the emphasis at the upper end on quality and at the lower end on cost. Greece is largely uncompetitive at both ends of the spectrum.

The country does minimal research and development (R&D) to create new products. Manufacturing under licence simply produces goods already available in the eurozone (where the workmanship is often better) without Greece being able to offer an offsetting price advantage.

Wages are about a fifth to a quarter below the EU norm but the non-wage costs (contributions for pensions, health, unemployment benefit etc) can equal just over half again the wage bill, forcing up exporters' prices to eurozone levels or higher. In those cases where there might be a modest price gain from lower wages, the differential is eaten up by transport costs.

The concentration on goods in this discussion overlooks the fact that Greece has significant exports of services, indeed the highest proportion of services to total exports (66.5 percent) among the 30 member nations of the OECD.

---

[22] Defined as the Balkans, central and eastern European countries, the former USSR, Cyprus, Malta and Turkey.

[23] Particularly traditional Greek products such as textiles, apparel, leather and footwear.

Income from the export of financial services is expected to burgeon in the coming years following the rapid expansion of Greek banks into the Balkans and environs. Greek banks are targeting up to a third of their total earnings from foreign ventures by the end of this decade.

Tourism receipts offset about a third of the goods trade deficit and shipping receipts cover approximately another 40 percent. But shipping is cyclical. And tourism is beginning to suffer from the same problem that plagues industry. The product - sun, sea and sand - has not evolved, while prices have increased to meet higher wage bills.

Similar products to those on offer in Greece are available in countries of the surrounding area - Turkey, Egypt, Morocco, Croatia, Bulgaria - at considerably cheaper prices, with the result that traditional package tourists are beginning to look elsewhere.

An effort is being made to create a diversified product that will attract higher value added tourists for things like conferences, sports (golf, tennis etc) and city breaks. But progress has been very slow.

In the wake of the Olympic Games, the tourism sector has been growing in terms of arrivals by around 7 percent a year, but the World Travel and Tourism Council - which does a rolling forecast covering a decade - suggests that the growth rate in Greece to 2016 will average under 4 percent, ranking the country in the bottom quartile of the 174 countries that it surveys.

The last Pasok and the present ND governments have bragged - and rightly so - about Greece's rapid GDP growth in the course of this decade. What they have not addressed satisfactorily is how to sustain this growth in the years to come.

GDP has been buoyed by the one-off impetus of the Olympic Games and by the foreign aid emanating from the European Union under the Community Support Frameworks.

Public investment is constrained by the need to balance the budget and the heavy cost of servicing the existing massive public debt that is estimated to be equal to just over 104 percent of GDP.

Private investment is strong, but could be considerably greater if the investment climate were right. Currently, it is held back by bureaucracy, corruption and a relatively high and exceedingly non-transparent tax regime.

Foreign direct investment as a percentage of gross fixed capital formation is, according to Eurostat, the lowest in the EU, averaging just 2.7 percent a year during the period 2003-05.

The high and growing current account deficit is cancelling out the benefit of the structural fund aid. An IMF analysis of the current account suggests that the deficit level in excess of 12 percent of GDP (recorded according to balance of payments data) does not accurately reflect the true extent of trade since not all the funds generated from trade are intermediated through the domestic banking system.

The IMF calculates that the underlying deficit is in fact of the order of 6.3 percent of GDP but at the same time concludes that the sustainable level is just 3.9 percent.[24] In other words, significant reforms are necessary in order to make Greek products and services competitive.

The following chapters attempt to assess the success of the efforts of the ND administration in the course of the past two years.

---

[24] *Anastassios Gagales, Marco Rossi and Marialuz Moreno Badia, "Greece's Competitiveness Deficit: How big is it and how could it be unwound?" Selected Issues, International Monetary Fund, Washington, DC, December 19, 2006.*

International rankings

G REECE fares poorly in the rankings of international agencies that assess economic and business competitiveness.

Two of the three principal annual surveys place Greece well below the median. *Doing Business*, prepared by the World Bank,[1] ranks Greece 109th of 175 countries, while *The World Competitiveness Yearbook*, produced by the Swiss-based International Institute for Management Development (IMD),[2] places the country 36th out of 55. Only *World Competitiveness Report*, the survey of the Swiss-based World Economic Forum (WEF),[3] places Greece close to the upper third at 47th of 125.

The country does slightly better when it is just the business context that is under scrutiny. The *Business Environment Rankings* model of the Economist Intelligence Unit[4] ranks Greece 44th out of 82 countries,[5] with a qualitative assessment of "moderate", which the EIU assigns only to three other EU countries - Italy, Bulgaria and Romania. The others are described as "good" or "very good". The *Business Competitiveness Index* of the WEF[6] puts the country 49th out of 121, just shy of fourth decile.

These assessments are dependent upon the definition of the criteria used for judgement. For example, the IMD survey under the heading "University education meets the needs of a competitive economy" ranks Greece dead last, while the WEF, using a different set of variables, gives the country a score of 4.78 out of six which ranks it just short of the second decile.

More instructive perhaps is the fact that, no matter how the criteria are defined, when they are aggregated Greece comes last among the 13 nations of the eurozone in all the surveys and close to the bottom of the league table of the 27 states of the broader EU, usually trailed only by some of the weaker of the recent enlargement states such as Poland or Romania.

[1] Doing Business 2007, *World Bank, Washington, DC, September 2006.*
[2] World Competitiveness Yearbook, *International Institute for Management Development, Lausanne, May 10, 2007.*
[3] World Competitiveness Report 2006-07, *World Economic Forum, Davos, September 26, 2006.*
[4] Country Forecast, European Union, *Economist Intelligence Unit, London, June 2007.*
[5] *In the EU27, this places Greece just above Romania (49) and Bulgaria (50).*
[6] World Competitiveness Report 2006-07

Table 3. Greek competitiveness and business environment rankings

Organisation	Survey	No of countries assessed	Greek ranking
Economic competitiveness			
World Economic Forum (WEF), Davos, Switzerland	World Competitiveness Report 2006-2007	125	47
International Institute for Management Development (IMD), Lausanne, Switzerland	World Competitiveness Yearbook 2007	55	36
World Bank, Washington, DC, US	Doing Business 2007	175	109
Business environment			
World Economic Forum, Davos, Switzerland	The Business Competitiveness Index, World Competitiveness Report 2006-2007	121	49
Economist Intelligence Unit, London, UK	Business Environment Ranking, Country Forecast (EU), June 2007	82	44

Sources: as listed

The most pragmatic of the surveys is the *Doing Business* report of the World Bank. It takes a hands-on approach, dividing business activity into nine subcategories such as starting up, hiring workers, obtaining credit, enforcing contracts and paying taxes. For each category, it itemises the number of procedures to be followed, the length of time it takes to accomplish them and the cost of compliance. These are then aggregated to produce a ranking.

Depressingly, under the global heading "Ease of doing business", Greece is ranked 109th out of 175 (up from 111th in 2006) while all the remainder of Greece's eurozone partners come within the top 40.[7]

---

[7] *Greece stands 69 places behind the next least efficient eurozone nation. Portugal, which is ranked at 40.*

The World Bank estimates that in 2006 it required around €22,000 to start a company with the potential entrepreneur having to take 38 days to complete 15 procedures. That makes the situation in Greece worse than that prevailing in many third world countries, let alone among its peers in the eurozone.

Obtaining licences is also tedious and costly. *Doing Business 2007* calculates the average number of procedures to be 17, taking 176 days to accomplish at a cost of approximately $13,500 (€10,800) in 2007 prices. To register a property requires 12 procedures over 23 days at a cost of 3.8 percent of the property value.

That is to say that to acquire the permissions to start a business, to register the property and to obtain the licences - a small entrepreneur must have additional resources equal to, or greater than, the legal start-up capital.

Once the business is up and running, the World Bank calculates that Greece has among the world's most difficult employment regimes. Using a series of indices ranging from zero to 100 - where the higher the value the more rigid the regulations - Greece scores 80 on the rigidity of working hours, 58 on the rigidity of employment index, 50 on the difficulty of firing and 44 on the difficulty of hiring. Overall, this gives Greece a score of 66 which ranks it 166th out of the 175 countries reviewed.

Enforcing contracts requires up to 22 separate procedures, taking 730 days to complete and absorbing up to 12.7 percent of the value of the claim, while paying taxes (direct and indirect) requires 33 separate payments taking 204 hours to accomplish and absorbing 60.2 percent of total profits if all of them are paid.[8]

Doing Business 2007 suggests that one of the reasons that Greek international trade is sluggish is the amount of paper work necessary. It estimates that it takes seven documents and 29 days to complete an export transaction and 11 documents and 34 days an import.

---

[8] *The World Bank estimates the black economy to be equivalent to 28.6 percent of recorded GDP, estimated in 2006 to be equal to €195.3bn. ie the black economy is estimated to be equivalent to €55.8bn.*

When it comes to winding up a business, the World Bank calculates that the process can take some two years and cost around 9 percent of the total estate under liquidation. It estimates the average recovery rate at 46.3 cents on the dollar.

Comparison of the situation in Greece with that in the 30 nations of the OECD reveals that it takes nearly twice as long and is nearly four times as costly to start a business. It is roughly twice as difficult to hire new staff and doubly costly to shed them. Taxes (direct and indirect) cumulatively cost about a third more than the OECD norm, largely because of high rates of social security contributions.

It takes more than twice as long to complete an export or an import transaction as it does on average in the OECD. Freight rates to and from Greece (using the US$ per container rate as the benchmark) are nearly two-thirds as much again.

Protection of investors in the stock market is very poor relative to the OECD norm and, should a business fail, creditors are likely to get back only around 60 percent of what they might expect in other OECD countries.

In short, doing business in Greece is at least doubly difficult compared with doing business within the OECD and considerably more so compared with doing business in other eurozone states.

Table 4. Ease of doing business in Greece

(Adjusted ranking compared with 175 nations)[a]

Category	2005	2006
Ease of doing business	111	109
Starting a business	134	140
Dealing with licences	53	55
Employment of workers	166	166
Registering a property	146	94
Getting credit	76	83
Protecting investors	156	156
Paying taxes	100	108
Trading across borders	119	123
Enforcing contracts	48	48
Closing a business	33	34

[a] *Adjusted to cover 175 countries. Initially ranked according to 155 nations.*
Source: *Doing Business 2006 & 2007,* **World Bank**

Table 5. Ease of doing business: Greece compared with the OECD

Category	2005[a]		2006[b]	
	Greece	OECD	Greece	OECD
Starting a business				
Procedures (number)	15.0	6.5	15.0	6.2
Time (days)	38.0	19.5	38.0	16.6
Cost (percent of income per capita)	24.6	6.8	24.2	5.3
Minimum capital (percent of income per capita)	121.4	41.0	116.0	36.1
Dealing with licences				
Procedures (number)	17	14.1	17	14.0
Time (days)	176	146.9	71.9	149.5
Cost (percent of income per capita)	71.9	75.1	68.8	72.0
Employing workers				
Difficulty of hiring index (0-100)	78.0	30.1	44.0	27.0
Rigidity of hours index (0-100)	80.0	49.6	80.0	45.2
Difficulty of firing index (0-100)	40.0	27.4	50.0	27.4
Rigidity of employment index (0-100)	66.0	35.8	58.0	33.3
Non-wage labour cost[c] (percent of salary)	30.0	20.7	31.0	21.4
Firing cost (weeks of wages)	68.8	35.1	69.0	31.3
Registering property				
Procedures (number)	12.0	4.7	12.0	4.7
Time (days)	23.0	32.2	23.0	31.8
Cost (percent of property value)	13.7	4.8	3.8	4.3
Getting credit				
Strength of legal rights index (0-10)	3.0	6.3	3.0	6.3
Depth of credit information index (0-6)	4.0	5.0	4.0	5.0
Public registry coverage (percent adults)	0.0	7.5	0.0	8.4
Private bureau coverage (percent adults)	17.7	59.0	37.5	60.8
Protecting investors				
Disclosure index (0-10)	1.0	6.1	1.0	6.3
Director liability index (0-10)	4.0	5.1	3.0	5.0
Ease of shareholder suits index (0-10)	5.0	6.6	5.0	6.6
Investor protection index (0-10)	3.3	5.9	3.0	6.0
Paying taxes				
Payments (number)	32.0	16.3	33.0	15.3
Time (hours)	204.0	197.2	204.0	202.9
Total tax payable (percent gross profit)	47.9	45.4	60.2	47.8
-profit tax	-	-	21.4	20.7

Category	2005[a]		2006[b]	
	Greece	OECD	Greece	OECD
-labour tax and contributions	-	-	36.2	23.7
-other taxes	-	-	2.6	3.5
Trading across borders				
Documents for export (number)	7.0	5.3	7.0	4.8
Signatures for export (number)	6.0	3.2	-	-
Time to export (days)	29.0	12.6	29.0	10.57
Cost to export (US$ per container)	-	-	$1,328.0	$811.0
Documents to import (number)	11.0	6.9	11.0	5.9
Signatures to import	9.0	3.3	-	-
Time to import (days)	34.0	14.0	34.0	12.2
Cost to import (US$ per container)	-	-	$1,443.0	$883.0
Enforcing contracts				
Procedures	14.0	19.5	22.0	22.2
Time (days)	151.0	225.7	730.0	351.2
Cost (percent of debt)	12.7	10.6	12.7	11.2
Closing a business				
Time (years)	2.0	1.5	1.9	1.4
Cost (percent of estate)	9.0	7.4	9.0	7.1
Recovery rate (cents on the dollar)	46.0	73.8	46.3	74.0
Memo item				
Gross national income per capita	$16,610		$19,670	

[a]Doing Business 2006 [b]Doing Business 2007 [c]*Formerly characterised as the "hiring cost".*
Source: World Bank

As a consequence, Greece does poorly in attracting foreign direct investment. According to data from the OECD aggregated for the period 2002-05, the country ranked last among the 30 member states in terms of inflows and number 23 in terms of outflows.

Its stock of inward FDI stood at US$28.5bn in 2004, just under 0.4 percent of the $7,337.5bn invested in the 30 nations taken together.[9] Outward investments in the same stood at $13.8bn, or 0.2 percent of the figure of $8,067.8bn for the OECD.[10]

According to data from the UN Conference on Trade and Development (UNCTAD) in 2005, the aggregate stock of inward FDI

[9]Trends and Recent Developments in Foreign Direct Investment. *OECD. June 2006. The figure rose to $29.3bn in 2005 but there was not an aggregate figure for the OECD as a whole.*
[10]*The figure diminished slightly in 2005 to stand at $13.3bn.*

was equivalent to 13.2 percent of GDP, while the outward aggregate was 6 percent. This made Greece one of the least extrovert economies of the EU. In 2005, the comparable stock figures for the EU15 were 33.5 percent of GDP inward and 40.7 percent of GDP outward.[11]

That year UNCTAD ranked Greece number 121 out of 141 in terms of its inward FDI performance, according to an index based on global FDI inflows in relation to GDP.

This is particularly galling given that the country stands number 36 in terms of its FDI potential, according to an index based on 12 economic and policy variables.

The difference between potential and performance illustrates the massive competitiveness gap in Greece caused by non-core economic factors such as political self-interest, excessive bureaucracy, corrupt administration, mismatched education and job skills and labour law rigidity.

Table 6. Foreign direct investment

	2000		2001		2002		2003		2004[a]		2005[b]	
	Greece	OECD	Greece	OECD	Greece	OECD	Greece	OECD	Greece	OECD	Greece	OECD
Annual												
Inflows	1.11	128.91	1.59	635.76	0.05	572.46	1.28	464.80	2.10	490.90	0.61	621.68
Outflows	2.14	123.90	0.62	687.66	0.66	619.10	0.41	612.63	1.03	781.79	1.45	716.06
Stock												
Inflows	14.11	4,241.78	13.94	4,582.87	15.56	5,262.60	22.45	5,321.92	28.48	7,337.49	29.31	n/a
Outflows	6.09	5,240.82	7.02	5,705.69	9.00	6,413.96	12.34	7,607.80	13.79	8,067.84	13.34	n/a

[a] *Preliminary.* [b] *Estimate*

Source: *Trends and recent developments in Foreign Direct Investment*, **OECD, June 2006**

Baksheesh

Greek companies pay approximately €34m a year in kickbacks to state officials.

The estimate is based on World Bank data for 2006 which calculated that some 0.23 percent of the turnover of Greek companies took the form of "unofficial payments" to state officials to expedite cases having to do with taxes, permits, legal issues and state services. Total company turnover in Greece that year was of the order of €150bn.[a]

Over half of all firms (55.91 percent) believed it was necessary to bribe

[11] World Investment Report 2006. *United Nations Conference on Trade and Development. October 16. 2006.*

tax officials, ranking Greece 11th in a sample of 27 emerging countries plus six western European nations used as controls.[b]

This placed Greece in a cluster with Azerbaijan, Kyrgyzstan, Tajikistan and Uzbekistan where "corruption is highest in tax administration".

Corruption was said to be limited in the customs service but "...significant in public hospitals, the police, tax administration and the judiciary".

Public procurement is also a problem. The kickback to get a contract in Greece was estimated at 0.79 percent of the contract price, placing Greece above virtually all the countries of eastern Europe as well as countries such as Madagascar and Vietnam.

"Stronger legislation and implementation is thought to be needed in numerous areas, including whistleblower protection, anti-money laundering, ethics rules and confiscations of proceeds in a corruption case", the World Bank analysts concluded.

[a]"Corruption by numbers", *Kathimerini (English Edition),* July 4, 2005. [b]James H Anderson and Cheryl W Gray, *Anticorruption in Transition 3,* World Bank, Washington, 2006. [c] *Ibid,* p 80.

Economic policy

THE NEW Democracy government came to power pledging not only to be a government that would produce policies to generate high rates of growth but also to be a spending administration that would boost outlays on key social sectors such as health and education.

In office, however, it has devoted the greater part of its time to restructuring the country's fiscal affairs while seeking to sustain high levels of investment so as to prevent an economic hard landing in the wake of the Olympic Games.

Because of spending ahead of the Games, real GDP doubled from an average of 2.3 percent in the decade 1991-2000 to 4.6 percent in the four years 2001-04 (*see Table 1 on page 23*). In 2005, however, it declined to 3.7 percent of which about 0.75 percentage points was attributable to EU transfers and another 0.9 pps to the external account that was buoyed by soaring shipping earnings. That is to say the purely domestic component of growth decelerated sharply to around 2 percent.

To sustain investment the ND government cut corporation tax, upgraded its subsidies under the Development Law and introduced legislation designed to attract private investment in public infrastructure through Public-Private Partnerships.

It also targeted maximum drawdown of structural aid funds under the Third Community Support Framework (CSF III), 2000-06, but discovered that this was more difficult than anticipated because of new programming and disbursement rules.

In 2005, the government was forced to repay to the commission €0.5bn that the socialists had spent without applying approved controls and in 2006 it had to reschedule €2.7bn in programme assistance because it had run out of time for disbursement and could not afford the national co-financing. As a consequence, Greece will lose around 6.5 percent of the total funding under its current CSF and about 5 percent under the next.

There is a real chance that it will lose more. At the time of writing the government still had some €13.6bn (42 percent) of CSF III funding to draw, spend and account for by December 2008, a seemingly impossible task given the pace of approved spending to date.

To buoy the consumption component of GDP, the government promised cuts in personal income tax but, because of the necessity to curb the budget deficit, these have been postponed until returns filed in 2008.[1] Contrarily, in order to meet revenue targets, the government has considerably increased indirect taxes such as VAT and consumption tax on tobacco and liquid fuels.

There has been some effort to contain expenditure but, rather than this falling on primary expenditure for wages, it has bitten into spending on programmes for social policy.

In sum, while macroeconomic results have been good, the government's performance in achieving them has been decidedly mixed.

Fiscal housekeeping

Pasok's last Stability and Growth Programme (2003-06) - published in December 2003 just four months before the March 2004 general election in which the party was defeated - estimated that the 2004 general government deficit would be equivalent to just 1.2 percent of GDP and that the budget would be in balance by 2006.

New Democracy declared this to be the product of creative accounting and, upon taking office, set about bringing on balance sheet large volumes of expenditure - particularly military spending - the recording of which the socialists had deferred by consigning the sums to debt, proposing to enter them into current expenditure as instalment payments fell due.

Moreover, the conservatives claimed that the socialists had been padding the adjustments allowed under the European System of Accounts (ESA) in order to reduce the general government deficit - the central government deficit, netted with the results of public enterprises and entities. The socialists' figures were estimates based on assumptions and not actual results.

Minister of Economy and Finance George Alogoskoufis argued that it was necessary to establish a true picture of the fiscal situation in order for the ND government to be able to make valid economic projections on which to base future policy.

There was a political aspect to the policy. It was designed to discredit the reputation as good economic managers of Pasok, which had overseen Greek entry into the Economic and Monetary Union (EMU), the eurozone.

---

[1] *Wage earners having tax deducted at source will have felt the benefits in lower deductions from their pay in the course of 2007.*

Ultimately, the ND administration lost control of the adjustment process and it backfired politically. The deficit skyrocketed, the economy came under surveillance by the European Commission and it was the conservatives who attracted the opprobrium.

ND's initial revisions more than doubled the Pasok deficit projection but kept it just within the threshold of 3 percent of GDP required by the Stability and Growth Pact (S&GP).

Eurostat, the European Union's statistical agency, which had long pressed Pasok to bring its accounting methods into line with EU practice, used ND's opening of this chink to drive a wedge into Greek fiscal reporting. A series of joint investigations between the European statistical agency and the ministry of economy and finance during the course of 2004 re-allocated deficit and debt allocations in a way that drove that year's deficit figure to 5.3 percent of GDP, which caused the European Commission to invoke the Excessive Deficit Procedure (EDP).

Repeated joint reassessments between Eurostat and the Greek authorities during the course of the succeeding two years ultimately drove the 2004 deficit to 7.9 percent of GDP, a record for an EMU member state. Despite Greek government objections, Eurostat insisted on carrying out a retrospective review.

The new analysis revealed that the Greek budget deficit had never stood below the convergence criterion that it should not exceed 3 percent of GDP, suggesting that Greece should never have qualified for the EMU. The commission said that there was no question of asking Greece to withdraw, but it tightened its economic surveillance, required detailed periodic fiscal reporting and gave the government until 2007 to put its budgetary affairs in order.

Luckily for Greece, two leading members of the eurozone - France and Germany - were also in breach of the S&GP rules at the time and used their political clout to change pact rules in such a way as effectively to remove all possibility of pecuniary sanctions for breach of the pact's thresholds.[2]

---

[2] *See Robert McDonald. "Swimming upstream". Special Survey No 58. Business File. Kerkyra Publications. Athens. December 2005. pp 14-18.*

Table 7. Deficit & debt according to Pasok & revisions agreed by ND and Eurostat

(percent of GDP)

	1997	1998	1999	2000	2001	2002	2003	2004	2005	2006
Deficit										
Previous[a]	4.0	2.5	1.8	1.1	1.2	1.2	1.4	1.2	0.5	0.0
Revised[b]	6.4	4.1	3.4	4.0	4.9	5.2	6.2	7.9	5.5	2.6
Difference	2.4	2.6	1.6	2.9	3.7	4.0	5.2	6.7	5.0	2.6
Debt[c]										
Previous[d]	105.4	104.4	103.9	106.2	106.9	104.7	101.7	98.5	94.6	90.5
Revised[b]	114.0	112.4	112.3	111.6	113.2	110.7	107.8	108.5	107.5	104.6
Difference	8.6	8.0	8.4	5.4	6.3	6.0	6.1	10.0	12.9	14.1

[a] *Pasok government budgets and* Stability and Growth Programme *forecasts.* [b] *Statistical Annex of* European Economy, *Spring 2007; figures agreed between Eurostat and the ND government.* [c] *General government, ie central government debt netted with the Treasury holdings of public entities and enterprises (DEKOs).* [d] ECB Convergence Report 2000 *and* Stability and Growth Programme 2003-2006 *(figures supplied by Pasok governments).*

Sources: Budget proposals, Stability and Growth Programme 2003-2006 and Statistical Annex *European Economy,* **Spring 2007**

The government reduced the deficit as a percentage of GDP by more than five percentage points between 2004 and 2006, from 7.9 percent of GDP to just 2.6 percent.

In part it achieved this by increasing Value Added Tax by one percentage point and by clamping down on evasion. But it also collected:

- €700m through extraordinary revenues[3] similar to those that it had complained of Pasok utilising;

- €416m through an increase in the percentage prepayment of tax required of corporations; and

- €316m in the form of a windfall tax on untaxed bank reserves applied during November and December 2006 when it found itself with a revenue shortfall at year end.

---

[3] *Such as special dividends from state-owned banks, extension of concessions, and rebate to general government coffers of fines and penalties assessed by the Greek National Telecommunications and Post Commission (funds that were supposed to form part of its autonomous finances).*

The government forecast that it would achieve a deficit equivalent to 2.4 percent of GDP in 2007 without such extraordinary measures but it made no real effort to cut primary expenditure (primarily the public sector wages and pensions bill).

The result is that that the central government deficit has remained high, in excess of 4 percent of GDP. The reduction in the general government deficit to below 3 percent of GDP was attained through significant increases in the size of the ESA accounting adjustments, reminiscent of the accounting tactics employed by Pasok and previously decried by ND.

The European Commission, nevertheless, accepted the government's accounting methods and in June 2007 the EDP was lifted. It also accepted the 2007 deficit projection. The government still faces the difficult task of fulfilling its commitment (together with all the other members of the eurozone) to bring its budget into balance by 2010.

Balancing the books

The government has reduced the basic rate of tax for corporations and partnerships (see page 60) *but to compensate has increased indirect taxes. In April 2005 there were steep hikes in consumption tax on tobacco and alcohol of between 10 percent and 40 percent) and Value Added Tax (FPA) was increased from 18 percent to 19 percent[a] (the preferential rate of 8 percent rose to 9 percent and that of 4 percent to 4.5 percent).[b]*

As of fourth quarter 2006, duties on mobile telephone usage were increased, while effective January 1, 2007 excise taxes were increased on liquid fuels. Greece has the lowest rates in the EU and the increase is designed to bring the country's tax regime on liquid fuels into line with EU norms. Further increases are slated for 2008 and 2009.

Also, effective January 1, 2006, VAT was applied on all new building works by contractors, though not by individuals. This replaces a transfer tax equivalent 9 percent on the first €15,000 of a property transaction and 11 percent on the balance[c] based on the objective value of the property.[d]

A Body of Fiscal Inspectors (SDE) has been established to monitor expenditure by central government, local authorities, social security funds, public enterprises and other public law entities. It has been given powers both to vet the lawfulness of expenditures and to oversee accounting of revenues and management of assets. Longterm, this is expected to help contain primary expenditure.

To date, though, the fiscal authorities' concentration has been on combating evasion. The Service for Special Audits (YPEE) was established to replace Pasok's Financial Crimes Investigation Office (SDOE) with a target of performing 70,000 company audits a year as well as conducting checks on goods trading.

The TAXIS electronic tax platform has been upgraded and the General Secretariat of Information Systems has devised eight ways of cross-checking invoices issued by enterprises. Similarly, a new system of cross-checking heating oil consumption against invoices for supply has also been initiated.

[a] This places Greece just below the average of the EU27 where it is 19.5 percent, but above that in the OECD30 where it is 17.7 percent. [b] The measures were projected to generate revenues of €1.1bn in 2005 (0.6 percent of GDP) and of €2.1bn in 2006 (0.9 percent of GDP). [c] These rates are reduced by two percentage points to 7 percent and 9 percent respectively if the property lies outside an area covered by a fire service. [d] Objective values are administratively determined property values set depending upon the location, age and condition of a property. They are usually below market value but are set by local tax authorities in order to avoid under-reporting of market transaction values when a sale is effected in order that the state should secure at least a large proportion of the tax that it is due. Objective values are supposed to be reviewed every two years. In March 2007, the ND government raised them by an average 25 percent, which meant steep rises in some urban areas undergoing regeneration, particularly districts in proximity to Athens rapidly expanding Metro system.

GDP adjustment

Member states of the Economic and Monetary Union keep their national and fiscal accounts according to a common set of rules, the European System of Accounts (ESA95).

The national accounts provide the measure of gross domestic product and are supposed to be updated every five years in order to capture new modes of wealth creation that have emerged in the intervening period. This is supposed to give a more realistic estimate for constant prices that form the basis for the calculation of real growth.

Greece adopted ESA95 as part of its initial efforts to apply for eurozone membership[4] but the exercise, undertaken in 1994, was conducted in a rush and contained significant lacunae. It utilised data

[4] *Greece had sought to join along with the initial EU11 in 1998 but, when it became apparent that it could not meet the criteria of the Stability and Growth Pact, withheld its application until 2000. It was accepted in March that year and joined as the 12th member of the Economic and Monetary Union on January 1, 2001.*

from the 1981 census (the figures from the 1991 census had not yet been fully analysed) and from the 1988 industrial and household surveys. The values given for various services were largely estimates. Nonetheless, the calculation lifted 1995 GDP by 23.4 percent.[5]

The figures should have been revised again early this decade to produce a new base year of 2000. Eurostat had requested member states to complete some 32 new short-term surveys to flesh out their data. According to the ND-appointed administration of the National Statistic Service (ESYE), their Pasok predecessors had, by 2004, completed only four and done nothing to revise the figures overall. From 2002, Eurostat placed reservations on Greek data.

The incoming ND administration launched a crash programme to update the GDP figures using the 2001 census, an industrial survey from 2000 and the household survey of 2004-05. Detailed new surveys were done for 16 subsectors, most of them in the tertiary sector, which accounts for approximately 77 percent of GDP.

The surveys captured significant increases in the value added from wholesale trade, the tourism sector (hotels and restaurants) and construction. The result was a further hike in GDP by 25.7 percent, taking GDP in current prices from its present level of €195.4bn to €245.6bn.

At the time of writing, the methodology used was still under evaluation by Eurostat but was expected to be validated by autumn 2007. (*2)

The OECD accepted the numbers in principle for its 2007 biennial report on the Greek economy, though it did not use them when discussing key ratios - such as deficit and debt to GDP - because of the policy implications with regard to the Excessive Deficit Procedure. However, the secretary-general of the OECD, Angel Gurria, presenting the report in Athens at the end of May, described the methodology used as "appropriate" and said that some of the Greek techniques used for sampling subsets of the tertiary sector might even serve as a model for other OECD members.

Doubters have questioned the magnitude of the adjustment but failed to take account of the fact that it effectively covers a period of close to two decades (from 1988) rather than the five years foreseen by ESA procedures. Moreover, the previous adjustment, made in 1994[6] had not been that much smaller.

---

[5] *Greece uses this calculation as a base year and calls it 1995 but, in effect, the reference year is 1988.*
[6] *Which updated many indices from a base year of 1970, a leap of nearly a quarter of a century.*

Rational assessment of the new figure was compromised by the fact that the domestic press - either by accident or by political design - initially presented the uplift as having come from the incorporation of the black economy into the recorded data.[7]

The confusion arose, it transpired, out of the fact that the ESYE had incorporated in the total uplift the results of a preliminary survey that Eurostat had requested be done by all member states to see what proportion of the black economy could be captured from estimations of untaxed sales of tobacco, alcohol, liquid fuels and narcotics. In the Greek case, this represented 0.7 percentage points of the 25.7 percent increase.

The head of the statistical service, Emmanuel Kontopirakis, says that by its very nature, the black economy is immeasurable, adding that his personal guesstimate is that it could be equivalent to as much as 35 percent of recorded GDP, nearly 20 percent higher than the estimate of the IMF.

Cynics suggest that the Pasok government had dragged its feet in undertaking the revision so as to be able to understate the value of Greek GDP during the negotiations for structural fund aid transfers under the National Strategic Reference Framework (ESPA).

The framework programmes provide aid to regions with GDP per capita of less than 75 percent of the average in the EU15.[8] In 2004, when the Greek negotiations were concluded, the average Greek GDP per capita stood at 74.9 percent.

Using the old GDP measure, eight of the country's thirteen regions continue to qualify for full assistance, while five remained eligible for transitional aid.

The new GDP estimate takes the Greek average to approximately 98.5 percent that of the EU15, above Spain and Italy and approaching the levels of France and Germany.[9] Had the new figures been in place and accepted at the time the negotiations were concluded for the ESPA, Greece would have been entitled only to about a third of the €20.4bn in structural fund aid that it has been allocated.

Brussels has not made any move to adjust the assistance in the light

[7] The confusion may have arisen because of the fact that the IMF had recently estimated the black economy to be equivalent to 28.6 percent of GDP.

[8] GDP per capita in purchasing power standards compared with the average in the EU15 which is equal to 100.

[9] If the IMF's estimate that 28.6 percent of GDP is not captured in the overground economy were to be incorporated, Greece would have GDP per capita of 126.6 percent of the EU15, making it the third richest country in the eurozone on a per capita PPS basis after Luxembourg and Ireland. This is one of the reasons that Greece is often described as a poor country of rich people.

of the adjustment, perhaps believing that Greece has had such difficulties in drawing down CSF III funds (*see pages 51 ff.*) that it will not succeed in taking up a significant proportion of those available under the new framework agreement.

Greece will, however, have to make higher contributions to the EU budget if the new numbers are validated since these are, in part, based on the nominal level of national GDP. The increased Greek contribution could be backdated to 2000; this would involve a one-off payment of the order of €2bn.

The new GDP magnitude will significantly reduce the Greek deficit and debt to GDP ratios. The 2006 deficit to GDP ratio will decline from 2.6 percent to 2.1 percent, while the debt to GDP ratio will fall from 104.6 percent to 83 percent. This makes remote the likelihood of Greece again being placed under the Excessive Deficit Procedure.

The wide variations in Greek figures of late - first on the budget and latterly over GDP - have made some commentators view Greek figures more as estimates based on policy considerations than as hard statistical data. Many believe that the real test should be cash flow and note that the government constantly struggles to meet its revenue targets while repeatedly testing its projected borrowing limits.

The latest OECD report[10] argues that this is why it costs around 35 basis points more to sell Greek debt than it does to sell German debt of comparable duration. Markets tend to focus on a country's debt service to revenue ratio and on this basis Greece ranks last in the eurozone with a ratio[11] of close to 11 percent, compared with Italy whose debt is higher at 106.8 percent but with a ratio of around 9.5 percent.

Table 8. Greek deficit and debt ratios compared with old and new GDP estimations

(Current prices)

	2000	2001	2002	2003	2004	2005	2006	2007
GDP								
Old GDP (€m)	124,388	133,105	143,482	155,543	168,417	181,088	194,902	208,740
New GDP (€m)	156,514	167,994	181,003	196,602	212,734	228,154	245,562	262,997
Deficit								
(€m)	5,089	6,501	7,074	9,554	13,110	9,495	5,154	5,102
Percent old GDP	4.1	4.9	5.2	6.2	7.9	5.5	2.6	2.4

[10] Greece. *OECD Economic Surveys, Volume 2007/5. OECD, Paris. May 2007, p 44.*
[11] *Net interest payments as a percent of current receipts (excluding interest receipts).*

(Current prices)

	2000	2001	2002	2003	2004	2005	2006	2007
Deficit								
Percent new GDP	3.3	3.9	3.9	4.6	5.9	4.1	2.1	1.9
Debt								
(€m)	138,758	151,869	158,887	167,723	182,702	194,666	203,190	209,555
Percent old GDP	111.6	114.1	110.7	107.8	108.5	107.5	104.6	100.4
Percent new GDP	88.7	90.4	87.8	85.3	85.9	85.3	83.0	79.7

Sources: Ministry of Economy and Finance, Directorate of Macroeconomic Analysis & Forecasting; Eurostat; *Athens News*

Community Support Frameworks

The Greek economy is foreign aid-dependent. It was the first recipient in 1947 of Marshall Plan funds to reconstruct postwar continental Europe. Until the mid-1990s, significant military transfers from the US[12] - including hand-me-downs of heavy armaments and soft loans for the purchase of new equipment - freed national resources for civilian spending. Since the mid-1980s, the EU has become the main provider through structural fund transfers aggregated first in the Integrated Mediterranean Programmes (IMPs) and subsequently in the Community Support Frameworks (CSFs)[13]. These monies have been supplemented by Cohesion Funds for the four poorest members of the EU15 - Greece, Spain, Portugal and Ireland - that have been earmarked for development projects in the fields of the environment and transport.

The EU funding is based on the principle of additionality, that is the community funds are designed to supplement investment programmes based on spending by national governments through their public investment budgets coupled with private sector investment and borrowing.

Under the IMPs and the first three Community Support Frameworks, Greece was allocated nearly €55bn towards development projects worth

---

[12] *The weapons were provided under bilateral treaties in which Greece provided forward bases for US military forces.*

[13] *These aggregated monies available through the European Regional Development Fund (ERDF), the European Social Fund (ESF), the Guidance Fund of the European Agricultural Guidance and Guarantee Fund (EAGGF) and the Financial Instrument for Fisheries Guidance (FIGF). Additional funds were available from the now defunct European Coal and Steel Community. Initially, aid funds sponsored by various directorates such as those for R&D and energy were not incorporated and were available in addition to the CSF funding. Latterly they have been incorporated.*

some €107bn. It drew down the bulk of its availabilities under CSF I and CSF II and these contributed between 1 and 2 percentage points a year to GDP growth. Under CSF III, the annual contribution was estimated to be around 0.7-1.2 pps.

Greece has had difficulties, however, in drawing down its funding under CSF III. The commission, concerned about the way in which monies were utilised under the first two CSF - not just by Greece but by all eligible member states - modified its methodology for disbursement.

Previously, funds had been advanced towards agreed projects under an *ex post* system. There was much backsliding in realisation and money frequently was shifted from one project to another, making monitoring and control extremely difficult.

To correct this, the commission drew up a new regulation,[14] which provided for an *ex ante* system so that, before funds were paid from the community budget, national authorities had to have made a start on projects.

To ensure that the funds were spent on the agreed projects, national governments had to have called for expressions of interest, evaluated applications, incorporated projects in operational programmes,[15] allocated funds from the public investment budget, called for tenders, made commitments to contractors, issued initial payments and applied preliminary spending control before they could make applications to Brussels for CSF transfers.

To guarantee that these were spent in a timely fashion, the new regulations introduced the so-called N+2 rule, which stipulated that any programme approved by the EU that had not given rise by the end of the two subsequent years to an approved expenditure claim would, automatically, be "de-committed" - ie lost.[16]

A government may already have committed all or part of its portion, but if it does not secure Commission approval for its claim for the balance

---

[14] *Regulation EC 1260/99.*

[15] *Under CSF III there were 11 operational programmes - (1) Education and Initial Training, (2) Promotion of Employment and Continuous Training, (3) Competitiveness for Sustainable Development, (4) Road Transports, Ports, Metro, (5) Railway Transports, Airports, Urban Transport (6) Rural Development, (7) Fisheries, (8) Environment and Natural Heritage, (9) Culture, (10) Health and Welfare, and (11) Information Society - and 13 regional programmes - one for each of the regions of the country.*

[16] *"Evolution of the budget execution of the Structural Funds, in particular outstanding commitments",* Communication from the Commission to the Council and the European Parliament, *Commission of the European Communities, COM (2002) 528 final, September 20, 2002, p 5.*

and spend it within two years of the original commitment it must bear the total cost. There is an extensive bureaucratic structure for control and auditing.[17]

Table 9. Community Support Framework Programmes[a]

(€bn)[b]	Total investment	Public			Private	Loans[c]
		Total	EU	Greek state		
IMPs 1986-92	3.2	2.9	1.8	1.1	0.3	(0.7)
CSF I 1989-93	14.3	13.0	7.2	5.8	1.3	(1.4)
CSF II 1994-99	29.7	21.0	14.0	7.0	8.7	(2.4)
CSF III 2000-06	51.2[d]	38.8	26.0	12.9	11.2	n/a
CSF IV 2007-13[e]	n/a	31.1[f]	20.4[f]	10.7[f]	n/a	n/a
Memo item						
Cohesion funds	8.9	8.1	5.9	2.2	0.8	–

[a]Numbers do not always add because of rounding. [b] European Currency Units until 1998, translated into euros at the central exchange rate of the drachma of Dr340.75 = €1. [c] European Investment Bank etc. [d] Includes €1.2bn in Community Initiatives, funds under the programmes of specific directorates. [e] Now known as the National Strategic Reference Framework (ESPA). [f] An additional €4bn in EU funds is available under the Common Agricultural and Fisheries Policies (bringing total EU aid to €24.4bn) to be matched with a further €1.3bn in national funds (bringing the grand total for the period to €36.4bn).

Sources: Community Support Frameworks

CSF III ran from January 1, 2000 to December 31, 2006. Contracts could be signed until the latter date but EU transfers had to be spent in an approved manner by December 31, 2008.

When New Democracy was elected in March 2004 - about 40 percent of the way through the 96-month programme - only about 24 percent of the total funds available had been drawn and disbursed.

The Commission for some years had been pressing Pasok governments to harmonise national legislation on tendering of studies and works contracts with EU competition rules and to change Greek methodology for project management and monitoring.

The ND government agreed that it would make the amendments but by the end of 2004 had not followed through. In December that year,

[17] For background see Robert McDonald, "Political brakes", Special Survey No 46, Business File, Kerkyra Publications, Athens, December 2002, pp 24-28 and Greece after 2006, Kerkyra Publications, Athens, 2003.

the Commission demanded the return of €1.5bn of the €5.3bn in transfers that had already been made.

After six months of frantic negotiations, the government managed to reduce the sum to be rebated to €518m. It also agreed to finance solely from national budget resources a further €220m in projects that had been supposed to attract co-financing.

The government has since been caught in a double bind. On the one hand it has been trying to cut expenditure to comply with the Excessive Deficit Procedure and, on the other, it has been seeking to maximise the drawdown of EU funding in order to sustain growth and prevent a post-Olympic hard landing.

Unwilling to cut primary expenditure, the government has chosen the classic option of cutting the public investments budget. In 2005, eg, PIB expenditure was slashed by 19.1 percent.

The government focused its attention almost exclusively on co-financed projects but, even so, the volume of EU transfers absorbed was considerably lower than planned.[18]

Table 10. Progress in absorption of funds allocated under CSF III

	2001	2002	2003	2004	2005	2006
Flow of public expenditure on CSF projects						
(percent of total of CSF III public funds)						
Annual	5.3	7.1	9.8	9.3	12.6	13.9
Cumulative		12.4	22.2	31.5	44.1	58.0
Absorption of CSF III funds						
(percent of total of EU funds)						
Annual	9.2[a]	5.8	6.1	9.6	9.4	13.1
Cumulative		15.0	21.1	30.7	40.1	53.2
Projects with a contract (percent of total)						
Annual	13.3	13.7	13.0	11.6	14.1	24.3
Cumulative		27.0	40.0	51.6	65.7	90.0[b]

[a]*The figure includes a downpayment of 7 percent from the European Commission.* [b]*As of March 15, 2007, 92.8 percent. The terms of the re-negotiation had allowed an extension of the closing date for the signing of contracts but not for the spending of funds.*

Source: *Macro Monitor*, EFG Eurobank Economic Research, May 2007

---

[18] *Transfers increased by 6.7 percent to €2.998m compared with 2004, when they had stood at €2.811m, but were 9.2 percent lower than their original target of €3.300m, partly because of a virtual hiatus for six months while the size of the rebate was negotiated. In 2006, they increased by 13.4 percent to €3.400m and for 2007 they were projected to rise by a further 10.3 percent to €3.750m.*

Under CSF IV (2007-13), now known as the National Strategic Reference Framework, investment programmes worth a total of €31.1bn were initially planned with €20.4bn coming from EU structural funds.[19]

According to the new rules, 60 percent of total public funding must be spent on operational programmes that are designed to make the country more competitive under the Lisbon Strategy, while 40 percent can be devoted to regional development.

The sectoral programmes focus on schemes to improve education, training and entrepreneurship, with a special emphasis on increasing the quality of public administration. The regional programmes will support local infrastructure and, as well, finance the new Development Law which is oriented towards regional development.

The government has drafted its operational programmes in such a way that they have a strong regional bias and the prime minister has insisted that some 80 percent of ESPA funds will be spent outside Athens.

The benchmark for a region to qualify for structural fund aid continues to be 75 percent of the average GDP per capita of the EU15, though there are provisions for transitional funding for regions that have surpassed the threshold either in real or statistical terms.

According to the old measure of GDP that applied when the ESPA was negotiated, eight of Greece's 13 regions continue to fall under the 75 percent threshold (Eastern Macedonia and Thrace, Epirus, Western Greece, the Ionian Islands, Crete, the Peloponnese and the islands of the north Aegean). These are known as convergence regions.

Three rose above the threshold on a statistical basis when the EU expanded to 25 on May 1, 2004 (Central Macedonia, Western Macedonia and Attica). These are known as regions that are *phasing out*. Two regions rose above the threshold in their own right and now have GDP per capita in excess of 75 percent of the average (Central Greece, the country's industrial heartland, and the southern Aegean islands, the focus of the country's tourism industry). These are known as *phasing in*. Aid for them will cease as of 2011.

---

[19] *When assistance under the Common Agricultural and Fisheries Policies is added, the total programme comes to €36.4bn, with €24.4bn from EU sources.*

Table 11. National Strategic Reference Framework (ESPA), 2007-2013[a]

in €m

Operational programmes		EU support	Public expenditure
SECTORAL			
Accessibility		3,700	7,400
Environment & sustainable development		1,800	2,769
Competitiveness and entrepreneurship		1,291	1,721
Digital convergence		860	1,147
Administrative Capacity		505	675
Employment		2,260	3,013
Education		1,440	2,215
Technical support		192	256
Territorial cooperation (3rd objective)		210	350
Total sector OPs		**12,258**	**19,547**
REGIONAL			
Macedonia-Thrace	Eastern Macedonia-Thrace (convergence)	480	738
	Central Macedonia (phasing out)	1,774	2,365
	Western Macedonia (phasing out)	421	561
Epirus - Thessaly - Central Greece	Epirus (convergence)	315	485
	Thessaly (convergence)	423	604
	Central Greece (phasing in)	367	734
Western Greece	Ionian Islands (convergence)	242	346
	Western Greece (convergence)	359	552
	Peloponnese (convergence)	313	417
Attica	Attica (phasing out)	2,438	3,251

Operational programmes		EU support	Public expenditure
REGIONAL			
Crete and Aegean Islands	North Aegean (convergence)	308	411
	South Aegean (phasing in)	140	350
	Crete (convergence)	423	564
Total regional OPs		**8,003**	**11,378**
Reserve (1%)		159	212
Grand total NSRF		**20,420**	**31,137**
Agricultural development		3,707	4,943
Fisheries		258	344
Total agricultural development and fisheries		**3,965**	**5,287**
Grand total for the period 2007-13		**24,385**	**36,424**

The full 141-page text of the National Strategic Reform Programme is available on the website www.mnec.gr.

Source: Ministry of Economy and Finance

By October 2006, nearly three-quarters of the way through CSF III, the government still had drawn only half the available funds and signed contracts for projects equivalent to only a little over three-quarters. To prevent significant loss of project financing[20] the Ministry of Economy and Finance negotiated a restructuring with the Commission. Its main features were that:

- existing operational programmes were to be revamped to include projects that had a higher prospect of being completed by the end of 2008 (€0.5bn);

- the EU contributions towards 2006 spending programmes would be increased (€1.2bn)[21]; and

- 180 projects initially slated for completion within CSF III would be rolled over into CSF IV (€1.0bn).

The first two measures mean that €1.7bn in funding will be lost from

---

[20] In June 2006 the government had requested a year's extension to the end of 2009 but had been rejected.
[21] The allocations appearing in the 2007 budget forecast have not been adjusted.

CSF III during the two 'grace' years 2007-08 and the third that the total amount of new money on offer under CSF IV will be reduced by €1bn.[22]

The government still faces the monumental task of spending 42 percent of the total funds allocated for CSF III (47 percent of the EU monies) by the end of 2008 while, simultaneously, finding the national co-financing to commence spending on programmes under the ESPA.

This means that there should be nearly a trebling of current outlays if significant amounts of aid are not to be lost from CSF III or delayed under the ESPA with potentially adverse longer-term consequences.[23]

Table 12. Public expenditure on EU co-financed projects (2006-08)

(€m)

	2006	2007	2008
Annual	4,500	11,700	11,600
Monthly	375	977	969
Of which			
CSF III	375	567	567
CSF IV	–	410	402

Source: *Macro Monitor,* **EFG Eurobank Economic Research, May 2007**

---

[22] *See "Progress on EU structural funding for Greece". Macro Monitor, EFG Eurobank Economic Research, November 5, 2006, pp 19-21, www.eurobank.gr/thebank/economicresearch.*

[23] *According to an analysis of the situation by the Economic Research department of EFG Eurobank: "[National Strategic Reference Framework] projects do not have the same deadlines as those under CSF III, yet if their implementation is delayed, it could be very difficult to gain momentum thereafter." See "Structural funding for Greece: The critical two years ahead", Macro Monitor, EFG Eurobank Economic Research, May 2007, www.eurobank.gr/thebank/economicresearch.*

Investment promotion

G OVERNMENT efforts to promote investment have focussed on reductions in corporate income tax and a generous subsidy programme, financed through the Third Community Support Framework.

Tax reform

In its electoral programme, the ND government promised to reduce the standard rate of corporation tax from 35 percent to 25 percent. The implication was that it would be done at a stroke. In office, however, it became apparent that revenue resources were sufficiently parlous that the cuts would have to be phased.

The government regularly spoke of reducing corporation tax between 2005 and 2007; in fact, the reference was to trading, rather than tax years. The reduction schedule[1] was 32 percent in 2006 on 2005 profits; 29 percent in 2007 on 2006; and will be 25 percent in 2008 on 2007 earnings.

These rates apply to Greek and foreign branch operations that are corporations (*anonymos etairia, AE*) or limited liability companies (*etairia periorismenis efthinis, EPE*). For general partnerships (*omorrythimi etairia, OE*) or limited partnerships (*eterorrythmi etairia, EE*) the 25 percent rate[2] was reduced to 24 percent on 2005 profits, 22 percent on 2006 and 20 percent on 2007 earnings. The legislation also eliminated stamp duty on profits.

For nearly a decade and a half, corporations had been permitted to create tax-free reserves of up to 30 percent of profits for re-investment, provided these were made within three years and the investments exceeded the value of the reserves.[3] The investments were supposed to increase productive capacity. Eligible investments included, among other things, construction, expansion and modernisation of plants and buildings; the purchase of new equipment or vehicles; and the financing of studies, training and patent registration.

---

[1] *Law 3296/04.*
[2] *First applied in 2001.*
[3] *The scheme had first been introduced for a period of two years in 1990 by the last ND government and was renewed every two years by successive governments with minor modifications to which companies qualified and the terms under which the investments had to be made.*

According to the Federation of Greek Industries (SEV), companies that had sufficient profits to take full advantage of this provision had an effective tax rate of 22 percent. SEV wanted to see it retained alongside ND's new tax corporate tax regime.

One of the last legislative acts of the Pasok government had been to introduce a new Development Law *(see page 65)* which included a provision increasing the size of the allocation to 35 percent of profits and extending the right to four years (instead of two) - until December 31, 2008.

The Commission competition authorities (DG Comp) objected, claiming that, as it was profit-dependent, not all firms could take advantage and, therefore, it distorted trade.

DG Comp said that the measure had not been notified for potential exemption and, in October 2005, it announced that it was opening an "in-depth investigation". It demanded that the ND government suspend the measure pending the outcome of its inquiry.[4]

The government in 2004 had already rescinded the socialists' legislation, arguing that the tax breaks available under its Development Law were greater. It did not, however, require some 3,500 firms that already had created such reserves to dissolve them.

On July 18, 2007, DG Comp ruled that the tax breaks constituted illegal state aid, and Competition Commissioner Neelie Kroes issued a statement saying that the ND government would have to recover a total of €200m in back taxes, plus interest.[5]

The same day the ministry of economy and finance issued a statement claiming it had secured agreement with the commission that 3,200 firms could offset the funds against the tax break provisions of the Development Law and implying that some larger firms might be able to use their reserves to make investments, provided these were compliant with EU regional aid programmes.

The statement nevertheless had a decided air of ambiguity. At one and the same time, it said "there is no problem regarding the returning of funds from companies that have made use of this law" and "the

---

[4] *"State aid: Commission requires Greece to suspend illegal tax exempt fund and opens investigation"*, Press release, *IP/05/1325, European Commission, October 21, 2005.*

[5] *"EU orders Greece to recover millions in illegal state aid"*, Kathimerini (English edition), *July 19, 2007. The ruling does not affect the tax breaks offered under the Development Law.*

procedure for the return of aid in the remaining cases will be decided after talks with the European Commission".[6]

The tax bill that accompanied the 2007 budget had foreseen the likelihood of a negative ruling from Brussels and included a formula that provided for taxed distribution of the reserves at rates of 6 percent for listed firms and 12 percent for unlisted. It was not clear whether the commission would accept this as a compromise.[7]

The general reduction in the corporate tax rate brings Greece broadly into line with the average rate for the EU27 where, as of January 2007, it stood at 24.2 percent.[8] The rate, however, is double that charged by the EMU's most competitive member state, Ireland, and considerably higher than rates charged in countries of the region that compete with Greece for FDI in manufacturing (Cyprus and Bulgaria, 10 percent; Hungary 16 percent; and Albania 20 percent).

Moreover, to compensate for the loss of revenue from the rate reduction, the government in 2006 increased the rates of pre-payment of corporate tax from 55 percent to 65 percent for corporations and from 60 percent to 80 percent for banks.[9]

Consideration has been given to increasing pre-payment to 100 percent across the board. This would provide the state with revenues to offset the cost of a phased reduction in personal income tax that the ND government promised for 2007-09. The Ministry of Economy and Finance argued that such a procedure would be justified in that it would treat corporations in the same manner as their employees who have

---

[6] Announcement regarding the commission's decision to recover illegal tax exemptions for businesses, *Ministry of Economy and Finance, July 18, 2007, www.mnec.gr.*

[7] *The distribution would have something of the character of a dividend on which, ordinarily, no tax is payable, since the authorities deem that a firm has exhausted its tax liabilities by paying corporation tax on its net earnings. Unlike some other European countries where dividends as well as earnings are taxed, the Greek fiscal authorities deem that taxing dividends in the hands of their recipients constitutes effective double taxation. However, as the re-investment reserves were created "tax free", to tax them at a rate lower than the 25 percent rate of corporation tax could also be deemed by DG Comp to constitute unfair competition (*3).*

[8] Corporate and Indirect Tax Rate Survey 2007, *KPMG, www.kpmg.com*

[9] *When a firm prepares its tax return (say for 2007 on 2006 earnings). it is required to pay in advance against the succeeding year's liability (2008 on 2007 earnings) a sum equivalent to 65 percent of the tax liability determined for the current return. This is then netted against the tax liability in the subsequent return. The increase in the advance raised some €450m in its first year of application. Law 3926/04 cut by half the amount of pre-payment of tax for start-up companies during their first three years of operation.*

their personal income tax withheld from their salary at source[10] and who must wait for a rebate if the deductions exceed their eventual liability.

In other measures to improve the tax situation of firms, the ND government in 2005 established a fixed schedule of allowable business expenses. This was designed to put an end to disputes about what constituted legitimate deductions. The scope for discretion in assessments by inspectors was reduced and fines for violations were lowered except in cases where intent to defraud could be proven, in which case they were increased.

In 2006 the tax authorities stepped up the pace of audits so as to prevent firms having to tie up large sums in provisions against eventual liabilities. Books are supposed to be audited within three years but a shortage of inspectors has in the past meant firms going without inspections for periods of up to a decade. Such delays both create uncertainties for the firms and obscure the transaction trail for inspectors in the event that irregularities are discovered - mutually disadvantageous both for the companies and for the fiscal authorities.

When in 2007 companies published their accounts for 2006, a number of large listed firms reported tax surcharges running to multiple millions of euros (€16m in one instance). In the main, the companies indicated that they were happier to have their tax situation clarified rather than pending - even if they may not have concurred in all the inspectors' findings.

The ND administration revamped the TAXIS electronic tax platform in order to increase its capacity for cross-checking of invoices with returns. Particular attention was paid to the collection of Value Added Tax (VAT). Firms faced fines if they failed to produce receipts with their returns and prosecution if they were discovered on cross-checking to have issued bogus invoices.

The authorities placed particular emphasis on cracking down on corruption within the inspection service. As of the beginning of 2007, the ND government reported that since it had assumed office some 60 tax officials had been indicted for alleged corruption and 40 of them sentenced to prison terms.

---

[10] *Under the new scheme tax began to be withheld from earnings as from January 1. 2007 and will be rationalised in returns filed during the first half of 2008.*

At mid-year 2007, the government announced that it would introduce new legislation to further crack down on evasion. A draft bill approved by cabinet[11] provided for among other things:

- stiffer penalties for tax officials who accept bribes, together with lowering of the limits which make the offence a felony that cannot be bought off with a fine;

- closure of enterprises for up to one month for serious tax violations such as non-issuance of receipts, refusal to comply with an inspector's instructions and "systematic" concealment of taxable income; and

- increased penalties for non-payment of VAT - including the blocking of 50 percent of bank deposits if the sums exceed €150,000.

To try to capture more of the turnover of service providers - among the worst for failing to declare their full earnings - the government proposed in July 2007 legislation that would allow individuals to deduct up to 40 percent of their taxable income (to a total of €8,000) for a wide range of non-essential services[12] provided that these were accompanied by receipts.

Development Law

Successive governments have introduced investment incentives legislation[13] providing cash subsidies and tax breaks to promote investments. All the laws have emphasised regional aid, dividing the country into zones related to their level of development and pro-rating assistance accordingly.

There has been only nominal assistance (eg, for investments in environmental improvements) in heavily developed areas such as Athens and Thessaloniki, while the maximum aid has been available for firms prepared to establish in border regions such as Thrace, Epirus and the islands.

Until recently, the incentives have been for investments in new ventures, although latterly there has been assistance for investments in modernisation and expansion of going concerns.

---

[11] "Bills in the works on tax evasion, EU funds, welfare". Kathimerini (English edition), July 19, 2007.

[12] Among other permissible services were restaurant meals, private tuition, medical treatments by alternative practitioners, realtors' fees and payments to household maintenance tradesmen such as plumbers, electricians and painters. See "Big fat untaxed Greek weddings". Kathimerini (English edition), July 20, 2007.

[13] See Robert McDonald, The Competitiveness of the Greek Economy 2005, Athens News [Books], 2005, pp 30-31.

The tax breaks have been generous, providing for reductions in taxable income equivalent to the total value of the investment. Few firms, however, have gone this route, because it requires detailed auditing of books and inspectors have not always recognised what firms considered to be allowable entitlements.

Most investors have preferred to take grants and to have cash in hand. Historically, there were difficulties with grants being taken and investments then not being completed. The laws were progressively fine-tuned to ensure that grants were only finalised once projects were operational.

The development laws have favoured small and medium-sized enterprises at the expense of large firms and critics have argued that the programme appeared to be designed with an eye more to political than to development impact.

Shortly before the March 2004 election, the socialists introduced their fifth Development Law[14] *(see page 61)* which tried to address this issue by offering extra incentives to larger investments of over €30m.[15]

The European Commission objected, however, on the grounds that this discriminated against smaller investors who, in most instances, were in greater need of assistance than firms making large commitments.

The incoming New Democracy administration abrogated the Pasok legislation and drafted its own Development Law[16] which set low investment thresholds and emphasised assistance to small and medium-sized enterprises.[17] The government argued that, as 98 percent of Greek businesses fall within the EU definition of SMEs, this is where the focus should lie.[18]

---

[14] *Law 3220/04 which modified and updated Laws 2941/01, 2601/98, 2324/95 and 2234/94.*

[15] *Firms making investments of this magnitude were to benefit from a 10 percentage point reduction in their tax rate (from 35 percent to 25 percent) for their first decade of operation, while firms making investments of over €40m were to see an alternative form of benefit - grants linked to the number of new work places created - increased by a third from the standard €45,000 per workplace to €60,000.*

[16] *Law 3299/04.*

[17] *The ND government drafted ancillary legislation (Law 3296/2004) which promoted mergers between small and medium-sized enterprises by exempting the merged companies from real-estate transfer tax and any surplus value created from income tax. The net profits of the merged company were taxed at 25 percent (compared with 35 percent) for the first two years.*

[18] *Under current EU rules, a micro-enterprise is one that employs fewer than 10 persons with annual turnover and/or an annual balance sheet of less than €2m; a small enterprise employs fewer than 50 persons with annual turnover and/or an annual balance sheet of less than €10m; and a medium-sized enterprise employs fewer than 250 persons with turnover that does not exceed €50m and/or an annual balance sheet total that does not exceed €43m.*

The ND legislation was in line with EU rules. To qualify, micro-firms with fewer than 10 employees needed to invest only €100,000; small firms (10-49 employees) €150,000; medium-sized firms (50-249), €250,000; and large firms (250+) a minimum of €500,000.

Aid was capped for large investments. Those up to €50m qualified for the full amount of incentive. For that portion between €50m and €100m only 50 percent was available and for investments exceeding €100m only 34 percent.

It took until April 1, 2005 for the ND government to get European Commission clearance for its new legislation and for the ministerial decisions to promulgate it.[19]

The ND law divided the country into six zones and the eligible investments into five categories. It provided for cash grants of between 15 and 40 percent, depending upon the region. In certain instances - for small and medium-sized enterprises engaging in activities deemed to be particularly desirable in terms of development policy - the grants could be topped up to reach 55 percent of the total.[20]

Alternatively, investors could opt for tax allowances ranging between 50 percent and 100 percent (that could be taken in stages over the course of a decade) or wage subsidies ranging from 18.4 percent to 48.1 percent (that applied for two years). These last were deemed more suitable for developments that were not capital-intensive but required significant numbers of personnel (eg, call centres).

The ND legislation gave greater emphasis to investments in tourism development and, for the first time, provided for assistance to supply chain services such as warehousing, packing and storage areas and logistics centres.

The Ministry of Economy and Finance claimed the incentives programme to have been one of its major successes. It received applications until the end of 2006 and their vetting was completed by July 2007.

The ministry reported that it had reviewed 4,399 business plans worth a total value of €11.8bn, requesting subsidy totalling of €5bn. It had

---

[19] As a consequence, there was virtually no investment incentives aid on offer for nearly 16 months from the beginning of 2004 until second quarter 2005.

[20] The commitment of own capital was reduced from 40 percent under the socialist legislation to 25 percent under that produced by ND.

approved 3,661, worth €8.26bn, with an aid component valued at €3.44bn. If all the investments finally come to fruition, they will create an estimated 21,281 full-time jobs.

The legislation was revised yet again in December 2006[21] to simplify it and align it more closely with the regional structures set out in the ESPA. This version[22] divides the country into three zones:

- A, which covers Attica and Thessaloniki;

- B, which includes prefectures in the regions of Thessaly, central and western Macedonia, and Sterēa Ellada plus the islands of the southern Aegean, the Ionian and Crete; and

- C, which includes the prefectures in the regions of eastern Macedonia and Thrace, Epirus, the Peloponnese, western Greece and the islands of the northern Aegean.

Qualifying investments are divided into two categories:

- (1) which covers targeted investments that include among other things upgrading the hotel stock (improvement of hotels of lower than two stars, conversion of listed buildings, addition of leisure facilities such as pools etc), diversifying the tourist product (establishment of conference centres, golf courses, marinas, spas etc), introducing broadband, promoting development of software, creating laboratories, and developing alternative energy (renewables, energy saving) and high-tech projects;[23] and

- (2) which covers more general investments in agriculture, fisheries, mining, energy production (geothermal, biofuels etc) and focussed 'domestic' investments such as central markets and abattoirs, social and cultural centres, and rehabilitation centres and accommodation for people with special needs; this category also includes aid for investments in upmarket hotels of B class and above.

The legislation provides two types of incentive (*see Table 13 overleaf*):

- cash grant[24] towards installations or wages; or,

- tax exemptions.

---

[21] *Law 3522/2006, December 22. 2006.*

[22] *For greater detail see www.elke.gr/investmentincentives/investmentlaw which provides a 17-page executive summary of the legislation.*

[23] *The legislation retains a programme that has proved highly successful in the past of subsidising two-to five-year business plans for modernisation of processing and products providing they are worth at least €3m in mining or manufacturing industries or €1.5m in the software sector.*

[24] *Or leasing subsidy.*

Small or very small enterprises (according to the EU definitions) can qualify for additional grant aid of up to 20 percent, ie the maximum for specialised investments in Zone C could rise to 60 percent, while for medium-sized enterprises an additional 10 percent of subsidy may be available in certain instances (ie up to a maximum of 50 percent).

Investment approvals under the new law "will place particular importance on regional convergence", according to a ministry communication.

Table 13. Incentives under Law 3299/2004 (as modified by Law 3522/2006)

(percent of total investment)

Investment	Zone A	Zone B	Zone C
Grants			
Category 1	20	30	40
Category 2	15	25	35
Tax exemption			
Category 1	60	100	100
Category 2	50	100	100

Source: Hellenic Centre for Investment (ELKE)

Venture capital[25]

The last Pasok government had tried to boost the high-technology sector in Greece by establishing a fund of funds known as the New Economy Development Fund (TANEO) to invest in local venture capital firms and by creating, using CSF III funding, a scheme known as Eleftho to promote incubators to take research from the lab bench to the development stage.

TANEO[26] was a public-private sector fund of funds capitalised at €150m, with €45m provided from the state budget and €105m raised through the international bond market.

The concept called for TANEO to invest up to 49.99 percent in some 10-15 new private sector venture capital companies that would specialise

---

[25] *For details see Robert McDonald, "Investing is divesting", Special Survey No 64, Business File, Kerkyra Publications, Athens, June 2007.*
[26] Ibid, *pp 20-35.*

in financing "innovative" companies in sectors of the "new economy".[27] The scheme was slow to take off and by December 31, 2005, when its initial investment horizon expired, only €38.5m had been invested.

The ND government restructured TANEO, secured permission from the EU to extend the investment cut off until December 31, 2008[28] and appointed new management effective January 1, 2007, leaving it with two years in which to invest some €90m.[29]

The new management claimed a pipeline of nine potential candidates including three domestic banks, one international bank with presence in Greece and five groups of individuals from the financial services sector.

As of mid-2007, however, the ministerial decisions governing the new terms of reference of the company had not yet been forthcoming and consideration had been given by the new management to returning capital to the private bond-holders.

Eleftho[30] was financed from the ministry of development's Operational Programme Competitiveness and was designed to provide funding towards the creation of private-sector incubators - firms that finance the startup of companies at the stage when new product concepts are being taken from the research to the development or early production stage.

Again there were several years of delay in getting the project off the ground. By mid-2007, seven new incubators had been established and two had already completed their investment programmes. Some 70 start-up companies were receiving or expected funding.

Because of the delays in startup, however, only around €52m of some €70m originally earmarked for the project was likely to be spent.

The ND government created a venture capital fund called Digital Leap,[31] designed expressly to invest in new ventures in ICT, information and communication technology. It was assigned €100m of CSF III money from the Operational Programme Information Society; this was supposed to be coupled with €30m from the private sector.

---

[27] Defined as telecommunications, information technology, e-commerce, biotechnology and new materials.

[28] "Authorisation for State aid pursuant to articles 87 and 88 of the EC Treaty; Cases where the Commission raises no objections. Official Journal of the European Union. C206/3. September 5, 2007. Reference number, N 133/07; date of adoption, May 16, 2007.

[29] The difference to be retained for possible follow on in existing investments.

[30] See Robert McDonald, "Investing is divesting," Special Survey No. 64, Business File, Kerkyra Publications, Athens, June 2007, pp. 57-62.

[31] Ibid, pp 54-57.

To satisfy EU funding criteria, the project had to be privately managed. There were prolonged delays in putting the contract to tender and when it was finally adjudicated in April 2007, all three candidate consortia were deemed to be unacceptable. The €100m in EU funding will now be lost to CSF III and rolled over into the ESPA.

Administrative reform

THE OECD, in its 2007 report on Greece, notes that expenditure on public administration was the highest among its 30 member states.[1] "Moreover," it said, "there is no evidence that the quantity or quality of services provided are superior, which suggests that substantial reductions in expenditure on public administration can be achieved through greater efficiency."[2]

It cites, for example, a 2003 study, which calculated that Greece could achieve the same level of public sector outputs as at present using only 71 percent of current inputs. This suggests that there is potential either for huge cost savings or vast efficiency gains.

The ND government came to office promising to "remake" the state, the implication being that it would both streamline the civil service and improve the quality of service.

Addressing the party's conference early in July 2007, Prime Minister Costas Karamanlis admitted, however, that there were still "unsolved problems and weaknesses" and that this remained his government's greatest challenge.[3]

He tried to shift the blame onto his Pasok predecessors. The state he said was "the biggest problem that we inherited from yesterday". But, though the government has instituted legislative and regulatory change, there remains a problem with execution. Procedures have changed on paper but in practice little has been accomplished because of the recalcitrance of time-serving public employees.

National Reform Programme 2005-08

In 2000, the 15 member states of the EU agreed the so-called Lisbon Strategy with the grandiose aim of making the EU "the most competitive and dynamic knowledge-based in economy in the world" by 2010. It set 17 quantifiable objectives in areas such as ICT, R&D, improvement of the administrative environment for business and mobilisation of public and private capital resources.

By midterm it was apparent that little progress was being made. Only

[1] *In 2004.*
[2] Greece, *OECD Economic Surveys, Vol 2007/5, May 2007, p 49.*
[3] *"PM wrestles with the state",* Kathimerini (English edition), July 7, 2007.

two member states had achieved more than half the targets, while most had attained only between one and five. Greece had achieved none of them.

In March 2005, the leaders of the enlarged community agreed to narrow the focus of Lisbon to the creation of jobs. The Renewed Lisbon Strategy, Partnership for Growth and Jobs detailed four areas for priority action: education, R&D, administrative reform and measures to facilitate entry into the job market.

As part of this, member states were called upon: to submit a National Reform Programme 2005-08,[a] which would itemise the measures governments were taking to implement reforms; and, thereafter, to produce an annual report evaluating progress. These would then be assessed by the European Commission, which could suggest necessary adjustments.

The Greek NRP represents a wish list and, as such, is a valuable document in that it draws together in one volume all the reform policies that the government would like to introduce. The first Implementation Report, published in October 2006,[b] is a frustrating document that reveals how slowly progress is being made.[c]

The Commission's assessment[d] said that, while Greece was advancing "relatively strongly" at the macroeconomic level, it was making "insufficient" progress in practical measures of reform.

Brussels expressed concern about a lack of targets, timetables and assessments and stressed the need for more attention to improvement of public administration, active programmes to promote jobs and measures to reform education (particularly tertiary) and to integrate it with market needs.

[a] www.mnec.gr. [b]*Ibid.* [c]Despite its shortcomings, the exercise of drafting the NRP was useful in that it catalogued in one document all the laws and measures being undertaken by 13 different ministries to promote growth and jobs, facilitated their cross-referencing and promoted modes of assessment of the degree of their implementation. A Standing Committee of some 50 representatives of ministries, special secretariats, regional authorities and NGOs assembled the inputs for the initial Programme and the Implementation Report, while the experts of the Council of Economic Advisors of the Ministry of Economy and Finance worked their contributions into something resembling a coherent format. [d]"Greece: Assessment of National Reform Programme", *Annual Progress Report,* European Commission, Directorate for Enterprise and Industry, December 2006.

According to the first *Implementation Report for the National Reform Programme 2005-08*[4], the government has introduced a new civil service code, strengthened Centres for Citizen Service (KEPs) and is developing plans to re-engineer public administration services. The delivery of e-governance has been made a priority in the forthcoming ESPA.

The *Code of Civil Servants* was introduced in late 2006, bringing together regulations on personnel management (including hiring and compensation), introducing a new selection system for managers and facilitating transfers of civil servants.

The code was drafted in cooperation with the Supreme Administration of Civil Servants' Associations (ADEDY) with the consequence that there is a tradeoff of fresh perquisites for more efficient practices. It does, however, improve evaluation procedures, introduce merit-based promotions and provide for transfers of public sector employees between services.

The functioning of the Centres for Citizen Service (KEPs) was expanded and they now provide online 20 different certificates required for dealings with state agencies and handle 18 transactions related to the services of the Public Power Corporation.

A new information system, e-kep, has been installed to link the centres with government departments to facilitate electronic processing. Conversely, the system allows central monitoring of their activities.

The government has devised a new policy known as "inter-service search", which means that public bodies must find by themselves 197 supporting documents that citizens used to have to produce in dealings with state agencies.

If an individual produces documentation that is mislaid by a public servant, it is up to the state employee to replace it within one month.

The Ministries of Public Order and Justice have each abolished four documents that individuals used to have to provide and replaced them with sworn statements.

In a moment of rare frankness in the text of its *National Strategic Reference Framework (ESPA)*, the government acknowledges that the reforms have largely been a paper exercise.

---

[4] Implementation Report 2006 for the National Reform Programme 2005-2008, *Ministry of Economy and Finance, October 2006. www.mnec.gr, p 40.*

"Unecessary [sic] workload, costs and upkeep of red tape, constitute a huge administrative burden and financial cost for citizens and enterprises... To address such weaknesses in public administration important steps have been taken as towards both the improvement of the citizen-state relations, and the internal operation of public administration.

"These are limited, however, to a large extent to institutional interventions (mainly personnel issues - recruitment, evaluation, advancement, etc) which do not always have any tangible results on the operation of public administration actually work [sic], or on the quality of services supply, and do not ensure public administration extroversion."[5]

The government has incorporated in the ESPA an entire operational programme - For the Improvement of the Administrative Capacity of Public Administration - funded at €675m. Pilot programmes are already underway in five public services.

Additionally, there are plans to revise the *Local Government Code* which, if successful, would greatly facilitate the process of securing licences and permissions. Local authorities are a major choke point in the process of establishing and operating a business and the snags are frequently finessed through bribes.

The Operational Programme Information Society includes a further €280m for the delivery of public information electronically and for automation of the procedures of the administration (including record-keeping and diffusion of legislation). The latter is supposed to facilitate inter-service activity.

Perhaps the most significant reform, though, has been one that has gone largely unremarked: the introduction of a *Regulatory Impact Assessment Report* for all new legislation.

Parliamentary procedure requires that policy bills be accompanied by a justification report and an assessment by the General Accounting Office of their impact on the budget.

The Scientific Service of Parliament, an adjunct of the Speaker's Office, examines legislation for its compliance with EU directives, the constitution and other laws and decrees of the legislative canon.

---

[5] National Strategic Reference Framework. *Ministry of Economy and Finance (www.mnec.gr). Athens.* October 2006. p 17.

Socio-economic bills are supposed to be reviewed by the National Economic and Social Council (OKE), but it is up to the discretion of ministers whether to provide drafts and the OKE receives less than half the bills to which it is legally entitled - often late, and sometimes coincidentally with their presentation to parliament, which compromises the potential impact of its assessments on ministerial decisions.

Parliamentary scrutiny of legislation is almost exclusively on political lines with the result that the incumbent government, if it has a working majority, can push through whatever measures it likes, provided it has the political will.

It has long been a complaint of the business community that new legislation is frequently counterproductive, adding layers of unnecessary bureaucracy rather than facilitating development activity.

In August 2006, a circular issued in the name of the prime minister required that, before presenting legislation to cabinet ministers, they complete a 12-page questionnaire to test a new bill's efficiency and effectiveness. The questions address such matters as whether the legislation might create new burdens on establishment or impact on the practices of those already in existence (eg, whether new quality or environmental standards might affect prices).

A special division has been created within the General Secretariat of the Government, which manages cabinet affairs, to scrutinise these assessments. Such evaluations have become mandatory for every primary law and secondary regulation and plans call for *ex post* assessments of the laws' impact.

Public enterprises and entities (DEKOs)

A S RECENTLY as the 1990s, some 70 percent of all business assets were owned by the state. It controlled utilities (telecommunications and water), energy (electricity, natural gas and the bulk of petroleum refining), transport (urban, air and rail), defence production, large swathes of the tourism sector (through the holdings of the National Tourism Organisation, EOT) and the greater part of the commercial banking system, through whose investment portfolios it indirectly controlled significant parts of manufacturing industry.

The privatisation programme, in train since 1996, has reduced the state holdings to below 50 percent, perhaps lower when part-privatisations of public utilities are taken into account *(see the chapters on Liberalisation and Privatisation beginning on page 122)*. But the state is still a major player in many walks of the secondary and tertiary sectors. The 2007 budget listed a controlling state interest in 10 part-privatised, stock exchange-listed companies (among the largest on the exchange) and 61 corporations and entities ranging from Hellenic Aerospace to Hellenic Festivals.[6]

Table 14. Selected state-controlled businesses

Business	Percent holding
Listed	
Agricultural Bank (ATE)	77.31
Public Power Corporation (DEI)	51.12
Hellenic Petroleum (ELPE)	35.49
Thessaloniki Water & Sewerage Company (EYATh)	74.02
Athens Water & Sewerage Company (EYDAP)	61.33
Thessaloniki Port Authority (OLTh)	74.27
Piraeus Port Authority (OLP)	74.14
Soccer Pools & Lottery Organisation (OPAP)	34.00
Hellenic Telecommunications Organisation (OTE)	38.73[a]
Postal Savings Bank (TT)	55.16[b]
Unlisted[c]	
Olympic Airlines/Airways (OA)	100.00
Hellenic Railways Organisation (OSE)	100.00
Attiko Metro (AM)	100.00
Hellenic Aerospace (EAB)	99.58
Public Gas Corporation (DEPA)	100.00

[6] *The DEKOs also include public entities such as pension funds, hospitals and universities but the government deals with these differently than it does with enterprises and entities having business-related activities.*

Business	Percent holding
Unlisted[c]	
Post Office (ELTA)	100.00
Greek Radio-Television (ERT)	100.00
Hellenic Public Real Estate Corporation (KED)	100.00
Tourism Development Company (ETA)	100.00
Hellenic Olympic Properties (OA)	100.00
Athens International Airport (DAA)	55.00
National Ports (10)[d]	100.00

[a] *Reduced to 28.03 percent on June 29, 2007.* [b] *Reduced to 35.16 percent on July 10, 2007.*
[c] *A selection of the more significant out of a total of 61 listed.* [d] *Alexandroupolis, Volos, Elefsina, Igoumenitsa, Iraklio, Kavala, Kerkyra (Corfu), Lavrio, Patra, Rafina.*
Source: Budget proposal 2007

In 1996, legislation was introduced whereby most public sector companies were transformed from direct dependencies of ministries into corporations that were supposed to function according to private sector principles as regards their organisation and operations.

But as the state continues to be their main shareholder they have been subject to continuing close ministerial control and, though ostensibly their employees are hired under private sector law, their unions have managed to negotiate contracts of employment that include dismissal provisions that are comparable to those for civil servants who have tenure.[7]

Employment in many of the organisations still requires approval by the Supreme Council for Personnel Selection (ASEP), which also vets the hiring of civil servants and state employees in the broader public sector.

The companies theoretically pursue profit and pay dividends to their investor, the state. In practice they are a major drain on budgetary resources. In 2006, they posted aggregate losses of some €1.5bn, with the lion's share of that being the responsibility of the Hellenic Railways Organisation (OSE) and Olympic Airways.

The DEKOs have massive aggregate debt burdens and the bulk of their loans are guaranteed by the state. The government claims to have been cutting back on guarantees but data posted by the General Accounting Office on its website[8] shows that the nominal amount of guaranteed debt continues to grow steadily.

---

[7] *Essentially an employee can only be fired for criminal acts or moral turpitude.*
[8] *www.mof-glk.gr.*

Most of the DEKOs have paid little or no heed to the notion of profitability but instead have occupied much of their time in fighting turf wars with ministerial departments and other DEKOs in an effort to justify their existence.

In December 2005, the government passed legislation[9] which, if it is fully implemented, could revolutionise DEKO operations.[10]

First and foremost, the law created a joint ministerial committee to supervise DEKOs. Previously, each reported solely to its responsible Minister, eg, OSE to Transport, EAB to Defence, DEPA to Development (which has responsibility for energy).

The Ministry of Economy and Finance (YpOi), while it controlled the budgets of the ministries, did not have a voice in the activities of the companies for which they were responsible. Nonetheless, the deficits of these companies had to be covered by subventions from the central budget and not from the operational budgets of the ministries.

YpOi insisted that, if it was going to have such responsibility, it wanted a say in the companies' financial operations. This, of course, impinged on their operational activities.

The demand led to a bitter battle within cabinet as the operational ministers fought a rearguard action to prevent any curbs on their autonomy. They sought to portray the Ministry of Economy and Finance as empire building by seeking control over their traditional areas of responsibility.

YpOi ultimately won the day in cabinet by craftily arguing that it was in fact ceding some of its financial responsibility to the operational ministers by agreeing to joint control.

A Special Secretariat for DEKOs has been established at YpOi with a brief to introduce private business practices into the companies' activities with a view to making them profitable and utilising their assets to finance their activities in the future. Many have large property holdings mouldering on their books at acquisition, rather than market, value and never developed to generate income.

The legislation provides that the post of managing director should be open to public competition and that the appointment should be made not by the responsible minister but by the DEKO's board of directors.

---

[9] *Law 3429/05.*

[10] *The legislation applies to listed as well as unlisted companies but the government confines its dealings with the listed firms to that of the controlling shareholder, that is to say it influences strategic decisions but does not interfere in operations.*

As the board members are government nominees, this still makes it likely that the minister's preferred candidate will secure appointment, although it should mean that the individual has at least have some degree of management skill. Whether these relate to the business at hand is another matter.

Contracts are negotiable for one to six years. Theoretically, a contract of over four years secures the post for the manager in the event of a change of administration - though the tradition in Greece is that even contract managers resign when there is a change of government in order to allow the incoming party to appoint its own people.

The legislation requires the management to draw up three-year business plans with quantifiable targets against which their performance will be assessed Their pay will consist of a combination of salary and bonuses that relates to the degree of realisation of the targets contained in their business plan. This is supposed to ensure that the plans are realistic and not simply fanciful forecasts.

The managers are supposed to introduce International Financial Reporting Standards (IFRS) which, among other things, require the inclusion on balance sheet of unfunded pension liabilities and the marking of assets at market of assets. New corporate governance rules are being introduced, requiring the appointment of internal auditors who will vet these accounts and report to non-executive directors.

Managers are supposed to negotiate new personnel regulations providing, among other things, that contracts of employment for new employees be governed by the hiring and firing rules that apply in the private sector (*see Labour on page 96*).

New hires will have to serve a probationary period before being offered a contract of permanent employment. The collective agreement will be the same as that for extant employees but with the suspension of special clauses that preempt dismissal.

The government argues that not only will this allow staff to be dismissed on business criteria but it will also facilitate the hiring of new specialist employees at market rates, instead of appointments being subject to ASEP rules.[11]

---

[11] *Some specialised public agencies such as regulatory authorities have in the past experienced difficulties hiring expert staff because ASEP limitations on salary levels have meant that there were no candidates for the jobs. In a number of specific cases, ASEP rules have had to be suspended before posts could be filled.*

The legislation provides that, if the company makes losses, the management can draw up new terms of employment and seek to negotiate them with existing staff. If they cannot be agreed voluntarily, then the state reserves the right to legislate them.

The government did this in the case of the Hellenic Telecommunications Organisation (OTE) after the management sought greater flexibility in hiring and firing following its massive voluntary redundancy programme that caused it to go into the red in 2005 (*see page 103*). But the government has not followed through with other companies because of the political cost. The trade union movement managed effectively to portray the measure as anti-democratic, claiming that it eliminated the acquired right of free collective bargaining.

Finally, the Special Secretariat is working on linking the DEKOs to the Management Information System (MIS) of YpOi with a view to being able to monitor the finances of the companies in real time.

The mechanics of the DEKO law are only gradually being rolled out. Whether the secretariat ultimately will have resources adequate to monitor details of the companies' finances or the political clout to intervene if it does not like what it finds remains to be seen.

If implementation of the legislation proves successful, it will be one of the most radical measures - short of full privatisation - towards introducing competitiveness into the public sector.

On past form, the inertia of the DEKOs will overwhelm the effort. The ministry will more closely monitor operations, but the companies will continue to operate much as before.

Theoretically, if the companies fail to perform to the standards that they set themselves in their business plans and continue to post losses, they could be closed down. For example, the Special Secretariat for DEKOs has identified as vestigial the construction companies attached to ministries - eg, OSK for the construction of school buildings and Depanom for the construction of hospitals. Potentially, they could be deemed redundant and their activities reassigned to the private sector.

However, in another act typifying the lack of coordination between government departments, the Special Secretariat for Public-Private Partnerships has accepted the nomination of these companies by their respective ministries as the contracting agencies for some of the larger proposed PPP projects.

Entrepreneurship

OF THOSE in work outside agriculture, 28.5 percent of Greeks are self-employed. This implies that Greeks have the highest propensity for entrepreneurship in the EU - on a par with that in the US.

The OECD, however, questions the validity of this interpretation. In its 2005 report on the Greek economy it speaks of the high degree of "necessity entrepreneurship" - people working for themselves because there are no jobs available - given that those in work have high security and limited scope for mobility.

The OECD describes the percentage of business startups having "high potential" as small and says that the net birth rate of enterprises - startups versus closures in any one year - is low.

Business registration

In 2001, the last Pasok government passed legislation[1] that was designed to reduce the number of procedures necessary to register a company to seven from 13 and to cut the time it took to incorporate a company from 50 days to one week.[2]

But in 2005 the OECD noted that to get an operating licence still required a further 16 procedures, adding that the number of administrative steps to be followed before the first employee could be hired[3] was the highest of any country in the EU19[4] after Sweden.

The report spoke of the lengthy shuffle of documents between prefectural offices, notaries and tax authorities and noted the high potential for corrupt practices to facilitate the process.

According to the OECD, the minimum cost of capital to start a limited company in Greece is the highest in the EU, €23,500, compared with the other extreme of a nominal €1 in the UK and Ireland. It costs €750 to register a company, significantly more than the EU average of €100.

The OECD acknowledges the Greek authorities' justification that the complicated procedures are necessary to prevent tax evasion on the part of the self-employed but ripostes that "...the solution is ensuring better compliance from the self-employed (eg, by more audits), not imposing dead-weight costs on entrepreneurs".[5]

---

[1] *Law 2941/01.*
[2] *One day for a limited company with paid-up share capital of less than €300,000.*
[3] *Or an additional worker taken on in a company already up and running.*
[4] *Member states of the European Union that are also members of the OECD.*
[5] Greece, *OECD Economic Surveys, Vol 2005/12, September 2005, p 89.*

In an effort to speed startups, the New Democracy government in 2005 introduced legislation[6] that

- abolished a dozen documents required to secure a licence;

- reduced the time for "unproblematic" applications from a year to a maximum of 30 days;

- stepped up the number of one-stop shops run by prefectures for registrations;[7] and

- eliminated establishment and operating licences for very small enterprises.

Despite the improvements, the 2007 OECD report concluded that "the number of procedures and the time taken for starting a business is still among the highest in the OECD..."[8]

Permitting a production unit

The reforms detailed above apply mainly to small businesses. Larger investments - particularly those with an environmental impact such as a mine, a factory, a hotel complex or an energy production unit - take considerably longer (two years and sometimes more) and involve contacts with a host of ministries (development, environment, transport, defence), state agencies and companies (the Fire Service, the Water Board, the Archaeological Service, OTE and DEI), plus local authority offices (regional, prefectural and municipal).

For example, to build a wind farm - and Greece is sorely in need of wind parks to meet its EU commitments for the production of electricity from renewable energy sources (RES) - used to require 39 permits that took three years to acquire.

In 2006, the government introduced a new RES law[9] that did not reduce the number of approvals but said that issuing authorities should pay heed to the initial permission given by the Regulatory Authority for Energy and take no more than 30 days to make their decisions.

The legislation was designed to reduce the length of the permitting process to one year (one and a half at most). The government trumpeted its achievement in spurring RES development, particularly in the area of wind energy.

[6] Law 3325/05.
[7] 53 have been established.
[8] Greece, *OECD Economic Surveys, Vol 2007/5, May 2007, p 32.*
[9] Law 3468/06.

Typically, however, the new legislation contained a clause that contradicted the basic intention. It required wind farm operators to include with their applications for pre-environmental clearance, a full year's data regarding the wind regime in their development area. The information had to be collected by the company applying for the permit and could not be acquired together with the land.[10] The requirement delays permitting by around 14 months and effectively obviates the time gained from speeding the other aspects of the process.[11]

The Hellenic Centre for Investment (ELKE) offers detailed advice on how foreign investors should proceed in making licensing applications. Its web page for energy was being updated at the time of writing but a précis of the 'accelerated' procedures that replace the previous 43-page ministerial decision[12] is given below.

Procedure for permitting a small hydro or wind power installation

*1. Request a **Permit for Production** of electricity from the ministry of development. This must be accompanied by, among other things, a full five-year business plan, a schedule for construction, plus cash flow forecasts. The application is considered by the ministry and the Regulatory Authority for Energy for approximately three months.*

*2. If the permit is issued, apply for approval of a **Preliminary Environmental Impact Appraisal**. This requires a detailed technical description, a 15-category preliminary environmental impact assessment, maps and photographs plus opinions from the Forestry Department, the Antiquities Department, the Hellenic Telecommunciations Organisation, the Civil Aviation Authority, the General Staff of the Ministry of National Defence, the Greek National Tourism Organisation and the City Planning Service with jurisdiction in the area. Consideration*

---

[10] In the UK, eg. sites identified as suitable for development come with wind statistics that have been gathered by the public services so that private developers have an idea what they are dealing with before they begin to consider the costly process of proceeding with permitting.

[11] There was a comparable muddle over legislation to promote the development of a biofuel industry to satisfy another EU directive which requires member states to incorporate 5.75 percent of bioethanol in gasoline and biodiesel in gasoil by 2010. The Greek government offered incentives for the creation of refineries but these could not be immediately implemented because of a contradiction in the law which required refiners to have contracts directly with oil-seed producers, while farmers must, under their EU subsidy scheme, have contracts only with oil-seed crushers. Application of the incentives was considerably delayed while the gaffe was rectified.

[12] Development Minister Decision 2000/2002, D6/F1/2000, Ministry of Development, Directorate General of Energy, Renewable Energy Sources & Energy Saving Directorate Section A, February 6, 2002.

of the application takes about one and a half months.

3. The environmental impact assessment is considered by either the ministry of development, its regional offices, or the local prefectural offices (depending upon size and type of investment) which issues a **Certificate of Approval of Environmental Terms and Conditions;** *the process takes approximately three months.*

4. If the investment involves change of use from forested (or scrub) land, the office of the General Secretary of the region must issue a **Special Administrative Act.** *This takes another three months.*

5. Obtain an **Installation Permit** *either from the ministry of development, or its local regional office, depending upon project type and size. This requires opinions from among others the Civil Aviation Authority, the Fire Brigade and the Centre of Renewable Energy Sources.*

6. Obtain a **Building Permit** *from the town planning directorate of the local prefecture, a process that can take between three and nine months. This stage involves payment of various taxes and dues, including, among many others, stamp duties in favour of the pension funds of the Engineers and Public Works Contractors and of the National Technical University of Athens and a pre-payment against future income tax obligations.*

7. Secure an **Operating Licence.** *This takes two months and might not be granted until the plant is fully constructed. To obtain this, the investor must have grid connection contracts with the Public Public Corporation and power take-up contracts with the Hellenic Transmission System Operator.*

The total process takes between 15 and 21 months but is much accelerated from what it was under the previous licensing regime.

Registering a property

Securing land for development purposes can be difficult because Greece still has no central Land Registry[13] and no National Land Use plan.

Property titles are entered in the name of the owner at 396 local registries.[14] Owners frequently do not register deeds in order to avoid paying property taxes and will demand that a buyer either accept

---

[13] *It is the only continental European country not to have one other than Albania.*

[14] *The description that follows is taken from [Robert McDonald]. Country Commerce 2005. Economist Intelligence Unit, New York, pp 26-27. For further details see Robert McDonald, "Building Boom", Special Survey No 35, Business File, Kerkyra Publications, Athens, March 2000, pp 14-16 and Robert McDonald, "Building Blocks", Special Survey No 41, Business File, Kerkyra Publications, Athens, October 2001, pp 12-16.*

unregistered documents or pay the tax liabilities associated with their registration.

A major project began in 1994 (financed with funds from the Second Community Support Framework) to create a Land Registry based on the plot rather than the person.

The Ktimatologio [Land Registry] Corporation was established to create base maps to identify land parcel boundaries and owners were called to come forward and register details of their properties.

Successive Pasok governments promised to have covered by 2003 some 8,500 square kilometres of the most built-up areas of the country and to have covered the entire 132,000 square kilometres by 2013.

But the incompetence of Costas Laliotis, the Minister of Public Works, Town Planning and the Environment (Ypehode) during most of the period that the project was under development, meant that Ktimatologio managed to register only 600 square kilometres by the agreed date. This, coupled with allegations of mismanagement of CSF funds, caused the European Commission to demand repayment of €100m in structural fund aid.

In October 2005, the ND government restarted the project estimating the cost to be of the order of €1.4bn. This was to be financed by registration fees.[15] George Souflias, the ND minister at Ypehode, has promised to cover the prefectures of Attica and Thessaloniki and the capitals of the other 49 prefectures by 2010 but has given no date for incorporation of the rest of the country.

There have been four efforts since 1976 to create a national zoning system, but each has collapsed under the weight of lobbying from interests who wanted to have their properties incorporated in the plan in order to permit their development.

The lack of an overarching scheme has led to *ad hoc* development authorised at the whim of municipal authorities who devise and maintain town plans and who are notoriously susceptible to pecuniary persuasion to have properties incorporated in them.

In May 2005, the ND government announced that Ypehode would create - by May 2006 - a National Land Use Plan coupled with three subsidiary plans outlining areas for development of industry, tourism and energy.

---

[15] *A flat fee of €35 plus 0.14 percent of the administratively determined value that is used for the calculation of property taxes less €20,000.*

The notion was to ensure dedicated areas for development. It was argued, eg, that there was no point in going through the prolonged procedure of permitting an integrated tourism project only to find that the adjacent municipality had permitted a power plant or a factory on its perimeter.

After more than a year's delay, highly preliminary draft plans were produced and put to interested parties for consultation.

The draft energy bill was produced in February 2007 with a promise that it would be put to parliament that April. (At the time of writing, August 2007, there was still no word of when it might come to the House.) It identified three regions of the country suitable for high-density development of wind: two prefectures in Thrace (960MW), seven prefectures in central Greece (3,238MW) and two prefectures in the Peloponnese (876MW).

The draft allowed that installed capacity in these areas could be twice what it might be in other prefectures but, according to RES specialists, contained fundamental flaws in its technical specifications that made the construction of wind farms nonviable. The ministry apparently has acknowledged these and agreed to make the necessary amendments.

The preliminary draft of the tourism bill halved the amount of property that a developer had to aggregate in order to construct a tourism complex from 300,000 square metres to 150,000 square metres and doubled the amount of floor space that could be sold as housing from 35 percent to 70 percent.[16]

That is to say, a developer, having aggregated a square kilometre (approximately what is needed for a golf course with associated housing), could, under the new rules, build for sale up to 700 substantial villas.[17] This would be ample to finance a leisure-integrated facility.

In 2006, there were a dozen such projects worth €1.5bn in the pipeline in Greece awaiting amendment of the zoning rules.

The new rules would, though, still require a hotel to be constructed as part of the complex; its size would correlate to the degree of development of the region in which the project is situated.

---

[16] Under the previous legislation, PD 250/2003, the minimum plot size was 300,000 m^2, of which only 20 percent could be built as a hotel complex. Of this, 35 percent could be sold as housing units. The remainder had to be kept for use as a hotel. The legislation was not utilised because the housing component was insufficient to finance the associated "leisure-integrated" facilities such as a golf course, marina or spa.
[17] 70 percent of 20 percent of 1,000,000 m^2 built as 200 m^2 villas.

Concern has been expressed that, rather than the legislation promoting a few large integrated projects, it will lead to the construction of many smaller developments with the construction of high-density apartment hotels. The rules would allow the construction of 350 apartments or maisonettes on 150,000 square metres.[18]

The tourism industry welcomed the draft as a "first step" towards the creation of a second-home market, but the environmental lobby insists that the draft will allow over-building that will lead to despoliation of the countryside.

A preliminary draft of the full National Zoning Law was unveiled at the end of July and referred to a national committee on town planning. According to a press report, the draft addresses issues that fall outside strict planning matters. For example, it proposes reduction of the number of prefectures and municipalities. (*4)

The report said that it places limitations on homes built outside town plans and bans construction on certain lands designated for agriculture. The draft reportedly was much watered down from the version prepared for the minister by a panel of experts.[19] The panel claimed that its recommendations were "backed by scientific data" but spoke of "a lack of experience regarding researchers and the administration involved"[20] (for which, read political concerns).

The calling of early elections meant that the main and subsidiary zoning drafts could not be put to parliament before the change of government. A new minister at Ypehode (more than likely even in the event of an ND victory) will mean further delays as the Souflias drafts will be, at minimum, modified and, more likely, overturned and replaced by a sixth zoning effort by his successor.

Company Law

The Greek Companies Act[21] is 87 years old and has been much amended without consolidation. In 2006, the ND government introduced

---

[18] *70 percent of 20 percent of 150,000 m² built as 60 m² apartments or maisonettes.*

[19] *"Experts object to altered plan". Kathimerini (English edition), August 6, 2007. A spokesman for the experts panel was cited as saying that the final draft allows more homes outside town plans, makes changes to recommendation regarding housing development on islands and reduces proposed cuts in the number of regional authorities.*

[20] *"15-year land zoning plan in the works. Proposal targets illegal houses". Kathimerini (English edition), August 1, 2007.*

[21] *Law 2190/20.*

more amendments that took nearly a year to make their way through parliament.[22]

Smaller companies with initial capital of less than €3m will not have to have their articles of association scrutinised by the commerce secretariat of the ministry of development but will be able simply to deposit them with the Corporate Register.

Firms with annual turnover of less than €1m will be exempt from audits by tax authorities.

The legislation gives added protection to minority shareholders. Individual shareholders are now entitled to detailed corporate information that used only to be available to those with a stake of at least 5 percent. The threshold is lowered for blocking minorities to demand an extraordinary general meeting, while just 5 percent of shareholders (or, in large companies, shareholders holding securities with a book value of just €300,000) can request a judicial audit.

The legislation permits the use of tele-conferencing and electronic voting for general assemblies and in some instances for meetings of boards of directors.

The bankruptcy law has been updated to allow companies to continue in operation during a two-year period of restructuring in hopes of preventing insolvency. Firms will enjoy creditor protection for one year; a committee representing creditors will have a say in the restructuring process; and a special court will be responsible for monitoring the process. If the company cannot be salvaged, procedures for putting the firm into liquidation are simplified and speeded up.

The new legislation removes the prohibition from a bankrupt starting another enterprise, a measure, which, in the past, made many entrepreneurs less venturesome than they might otherwise have been.

Red tape

Once established, Greek businesses spend nearly twice as much time as their EU counterparts filling out forms and providing data to comply with bureaucratic requirements. According to a European Commission working paper published in November 2006, the administrative cost of complying with state regulations in Greece is equivalent to 6.8 percent

---

[22] *"Bill will radically reform corporate law, enhance rights of minority shareholders"*. Kathimerini (English edition). *July 14, 2006 and "Amended bill on sociétées anonymes becomes law"*. Kathimerini (English edition). *July 26, 2007.*

of GDP, compared with an average in the EU25 of 3.5 percent.[23] In nominal terms, this is approximately half of the surplus value generated by business.

The European Commission is embarked on a programme, as part of the revised Lisbon Process, to reduce red tape by 25 percent by 2012.[24] It has identified 13 areas in which it says it will seek to reduce its demands for information.[25] A first package of measures, announced in March 2007, affected road hauliers, butchers, bakers and grocers. It also eliminated the requirement for experts' reports on SME mergers and divisions unless these were specifically demanded by shareholders.

A working document[26] calculated that if the EU targets could be achieved in Greece it would increase the efficiency of labour by 2.9 percent, improving value added as a consequence.[27]

Closed shops

The OECD in its 2007 report claims that regulation of professional services in Greece is probably the most restrictive among its 30 members. The claim is based on a series of indicators that the organisation maintains for the legal, accounting, engineering and architectural professions. It blames both licensing requirements and fixing of fees.

The government claims that it seeks to promote free markets monitored by strong regulatory authorities. It nevertheless allows restrictive practices in a number of sectors including:

- retail (shop-opening hours);

- pharmaceuticals (pricing and opening hours for drug stores); and

- transport (the price and number of taxi licences and tariffs for inter-regional domestic haulage).

---

[23] *The only other member states approaching this level were Hungary, the Baltic states, Cyprus and Malta. The European Commission describes administrative costs as those incurred by enterprises in meeting legal obligations to provide information on their activities or production to either public authorities or private parties. These are different from compliance costs, which stem from legislative requirements associated with the development of new products and processes.*

[24] *It is estimated that this could increase average GDP by 1.4 percent, the equivalent of €150bn in 2006.*

[25] *Company law, pharmaceutical legislation, working environment and employment relations, tax law with particular reference to VAT, statistics, agricultural subsidies, food safety, transport, fisheries, financial services, the environment, cohesion policy and public procurement.*

[26] Impact assessment, Action programme for Reducing Administrative Burdens in the European Union, *COM (2007) 23 final [accompanying SEC (2007)85]. European Commission, January 24, 2007.*

[27] *The cost share of labour in value added in Greece is estimated at 59.5 percent, compared with an average of 56.9 percent in the EU25.*

A study by the Centre for Economic Planning and Research (KEPE), published in Spring 2007, claimed that there were at least 70 professions in Greece - mostly in the services sector - in which some degree of restrictive practice applied.

KEPE calculated that if these could be removed, there would be a 0.2 percent increase in employment, a 0.3 percent increase in private consumption, a 0.4 percent increase in real wages and a 0.9 percent increase on return on capital, which would translate into an annual increase in GDP of approximately 0.3 percentage points.[28]

Price fixing

There is significant cartelisation among Greek producers that leads to price fixing, a major factor contributing to Greece's high level of inflation.

The Commerce Secretariat of the Ministry of Development has stepped up its monitoring of the retail sector (particularly of public markets) and promoted the work of the Competition Committee (EA) in dealing with wholesalers and producers.

The committee, established in 1995, has two functions: a) to deal with concentrations, and b) to prevent cartels and restrictive practices.

It used to concentrate on the approval of mergers and acquisitions with a view to preventing the creation of firms so large that they could control prices by dint of their domination of markets.

The OECD in a 2001 report on regulatory reform[29] said that, as most Greek firms were relatively small to begin with, markets could benefit from consolidation. What was needed, it argued, was more attention to price-fixing and other collusive practices that prevented competition and the entry of new participants into a market.

Following the introduction of new EU competition rules in 2005, which transferred a considerable part of the Brussels Competition Directorate's competences to national authorities,[30] the Greek Competition Committee stepped up its monitoring of trading practices.[31]

---

[28] "Greek economy to reap substantial benefits from the opening up of closed-shop domains", Kathimerini (English edition), April 21. 2007.

[29] Regulatory Reform in Greece, OECD, Paris, May 2001, p 68.

[30] Council Regulation 1/03 implemented in Greece through Law 3373/05.

[31] Under new legislation governing the "electronic communications" market (Law 3431/06), the competences of the Competition Committee to regulate the telecommunications and associated markets were transferred to the National Telecommunications and Post Commission (EETT).

In 2005 it slapped a fine of €15m on the Trade Association of Greek Supermarkets (SESME) plus fines totalling €1.8m on seven of the association's members for having colluded to fix the percentage of rebates to be included in the invoices of suppliers, with the threat of exclusion of their products if they did not comply.[32]

Previously, the EA had been a low-profile, rather introverted body. Under the new legislation, the committee appeared to find a new confidence, tackling everything from price fixing among dentists to restrictions placed by car manufacturers on the sales tactics of their dealers.

EA had even begun to undertake investigations on its own initiative. It had launched a preliminary inquiry into the brewing industry and was investigating an alleged cartel among the country's leading dairy companies when its work suffered a body blow. In September 2006, the director-general of its secretariat, Panayiotis Adamopoulos, was remanded in custody, together with two businessmen, for allegedly trying to extort money (in exchange for lenience) from one of the companies under investigation in the milk inquiry.

The committee stopped work on new inquiries in order to review all cases in which Adamopoulos had a hand and, from evolving as a proactive agency, retreated into itself once more. (As of July 2007, eg, its annual review of 2006 activities had not yet appeared.)

The one positive note was that in July 2007 the government announced that it finally would loose EA from the hiring strictures of ASEP, thus facilitating the employment of the additional 50 professionals, such as economists and lawyers, that it requires to fill out its undermanned staff complement. (*5)

---

[32] *For background, see* Annual Report on Competition Policy 2005, *Hellenic Competition Commission [sic], Submission to the Committee on Competition Law and Policy of the OECD, May 10, 2006, pp 5-8.*

Labour

I N THEIR analyses of the Greek economy, international agencies (such as the EC, IMF and OECD) regularly call for an end to what they describe as "labour market rigidities".

Historically, their focus of attention has been on the redundancy provisions of Greek labour law. These used to allow firms employing between 20 and 49 people to fire five per month, but those employing 50 or more to make redundant only 2 percent of their workforce.

Legislation introduced by the last Pasok government[1] made it slightly easier to lay off workers in large firms but tightened the procedures in small companies and significantly hiked the cost of overtime payments in hopes of forcing employers to hire new workers.

Firms employing 200 or more people were allowed to fire 2 percent to 3 percent of their staff each month (up to a maximum of 30) but those employing between 20 and 199 were limited to firing four.

The new overtime provisions allowed employers to demand three hours a week at 150 percent of basic pay (up to 120 hours annually) with any further overtime paid at 250 percent of the basic rate.[2]

Employers prefer to pay existing workers overtime rather than hire new ones when times are good for fear of not being able to shed them when business is slack. They claimed the new overtime rules added some 13 percent to their wage bill and made them uncompetitive vis a vis EU peers.

The Greek General Confederation of Labour (GSEE) insists the layoff rules are sacrosanct. For one thing, they are not wildly out of line with those in other EU countries. For another, GSEE argues, more than 95 percent of Greek businesses are small firms that employ fewer than 20 people. Thus the majority of employers are able to shed staff at will.

Table 15. Employment and unemployment in Greece and the EU13[a]

(percent)

	2000	2001	2002	2003	2004	2005	2006	2007	2008
Employment									
Greece	55.2	55.1	56.2	57.4	57.9	58.7	59.3	59.9	60.5
EU13	64.1	64.8	65.1	65.2	65.4	65.6	66.4	67.2	67.9

[1] *Law 2874/00.*

[2] *Theoretically, it was possible to get a ministerial authorisation for such overtime in which case it would be paid at 175 percent, but such permissions were virtually never forthcoming. For more details see Robert McDonald, "Stability and Growth", Special Survey No 42, Business File, December 2001, pp 26-27.*

	2000	2001	2002	2003	2004	2005	2006	2007	2008
Unemployment									
Greece	11.2	10.7	10.3	9.7	10.5[b]	9.8	8.9	8.5	8.1
EU13	8.2	7.8	8.2	8.7	8.8	8.6	7.9	7.3	6.9
Memo item: GDP									
Greece	4.5	5.1	3.8	4.8	4.7	3.7	4.3	3.7	3.7
EU13	3.9	1.9	0.9	0.8	2.0	1.4	2.7	2.6	2.5

[a] *Slovenia became the 13th member of the Economic and Monetary Union (the eurozone) as of January 1, 2007.* [b] *As of January 1, 2005, the ND administration of the National Statistical Service began to publish data based on a new labour force survey utilising data from the 2001 (as opposed to the 1991) census and a larger sample. The data are retroactive only to Q1 2004; figures previous to that date are based on the old methodology.*

Source: Statistical Annex of *European Economy*, European Commission, Spring 2007

GSEE has always claimed that Greece's labour problems have not so much to do with firing as with hiring. The benchmark employment rate in Greece[3] is considerably below that in other member states of the eurozone. In 2006 it stood at 59.3 percent compared with 66.4 percent in the EU13; by 2008 it is forecast to grow a further 1.2 percent (to 60.5 percent) but this will lag the increase in the eurozone of 1.5 percent (to 67.9 percent)[4]. Moreover, the differential in the rate of growth in employment between Greece and the EU13 has not been commensurate with that in the rate of growth of GDP *(cf Table 1)*.

Employment and unemployment statistics in Greece have always been weak. Under Pasok governments, the National Statistical Service (ESYE) used a relatively small sample based on the 1991 census. The new administration appointed by ND has updated this using data from the 2001 census and expanding the number of households interviewed.[5] Still, it was not until 2005 that the ESYE began regularly to publish quarterly unemployment statistics and only in 2007 did monthly figures become available.

The Greek stats do not properly capture economic migrants and

---

[3] *The employment rate as defined by Eurostat is the ratio of civilian employment to the total population aged 15-64. Persons engaged in obligatory military service are excluded.*

[4] *According to data published by Eurostat in its* Spring Economic Forecasts 2007, *published in April 2007. According to the Greek government* Stability and Growth Programme 2006-2009, *published in December 2006, employment is slated to grow by 1.8 percent a year in 2007 and each of the following two years.*

[5] *In first quarter 2007, 30,755 households, or 0.73 percent of the total number.*

persons working in the black economy. Moreover, there is significant underemployment of spouses and children participating in small family businesses either for no pay or at well below market rates.[6]

Bearing these factors in mind, it is still possible to make generalisations about the Greek labour market.

Unemployment has been falling but still stands above the norm in the eurozone. The Pasok methodology saw the differential in the headline figures narrow to one percentage point in 2003 but ND's new measuring methods boosted this to 1.7 pps in 2004, and it was only in 2006 that the gap narrowed to one percentage point once more.

Eurostat expects this gap to widen to 1.2 pps this year and next. The Greek government, which estimated 2006 unemployment to be 0.7 pps lower than the rate estimated by Eurostat (8.2 percent compared with 8.9 percent), forecasts that by 2008 this will fall to 0.4 pps below the eurozone norm (6.5 percent compared with 6.9 percent).[7]

The headline figures mask significant structural anomalies. The rate of unemployment is among:

- women more than double that for men;
- the young two to three times higher than that among prime-age workers (30-64); and
- young females nearly twice that among young men.

Table 16. Unemployment rate by sex and age groups, Q1 2007

(percent)

Age groups	Q1					
	2006			2007		
	Males	Females	Total	Males	Females	Total
15-29	13.2	25.5	18.7	13.2	24.8	18.2
30-44	5.5	13.1	8.7	4.8	13.0	8.3
45-64	3.5	8.5	5.3	2.9	7.9	4.8
65+	1.6	3.5	2.1	0.9	1.4	1.1
Total	6.3	14.6	9.7	5.7	13.9	9.1

Source: Press release, National Statistical Service of Greece, June 28, 2007

[6] *The ESYE estimates that 63 percent of those in work are employees, 7 percent are unpaid family workers, 8 percent are employers and 22 percent are own-account workers.*
[7] *The Stability and Growth Programme 2006-2009 forecast unemployment in 2007 to be 7.4 percent (compared with the Eurostat estimate of 8.5 percent) and in 2008 to be 6.5 percent (8.1 percent)*

Nearly a third of the unemployed in Q1 2007 (33.2 percent) were new entrants to the market looking for their first job; nearly half (49 percent) were longterm unemployed (persons who have been out of work for more than one year).[8] The relatively high rate of job security for those in work, coupled with a propensity of salaried workers not to change jobs, makes it difficult for newcomers to break into the job market and doubly difficult for those who are laid off to re-enter it.[9]

Collective wage agreements stress seniority as opposed to productivity, which means that the wage bill is pushed up by the preponderance of older workers.

The upgrading of skills is compromised by the fact that it is difficult to take on younger workers familiar with new disciplines because it is impossible to get rid of older workers lacking the requisite training (this is particularly true in sectors dependent upon IT). Lifelong learning in Greece is a concept in its infancy.

It is particularly difficult for women to work and coincidentally to raise a family because child care facilities are limited (though improving); those who leave to have a family find it difficult to return to the job market because there are only limited opportunities for part-time working except in relatively low-paid posts.

Since 1990, government has withdrawn from involvement in private sector wage bargaining, though its pay increases for civil servants set the tenor for wage rises in the private sector.[10]

There is a complex, three-tier wage-bargaining process. GSEE and three employers' organisations[11] negotiate a National Minimum Wage Agreement. It sets a basic wage for an unskilled, unmarried worker plus some 20 supplementary categories that relate to marital status, family obligations and length of service. The agreements also cover perquisites such as parental leave, vacation allowance and severance pay.

---

[8] The maximum period for which unemployment insurance is payable.

[9] That said, Greek workers are choosy about what work they will accept. According to the ESYE data, 88 percent of the unemployed said they wanted a full-time job, and 41 percent said they would not accept part-time work. Of the unemployed offered work, 12.7 percent refused the jobs available: 23.8 percent because the job was not suitable, 20 percent because the wage was not satisfactory and 17.7 percent because the working hours were not convenient.

[10] There is the possibility of intervention through the Mediation and Arbitration Organisation (OMED), though it emphasises its mediation role and only resorts to binding arbitration in particularly intractable cases.

[11] The lead is taken by the Federation of Greek Industries together with the National Confederation of Greek Traders' Associations and the General Confederation of Professionals, Craftsmen and Tradesmen.

Though only about 20 percent of the workforce is unionised, by practice the national minimum agreement applies to all salaried employees.

There is a second tier of negotiations at the level of union federation (such as electricians) or branch of economic activity (such as banking). These produce increments related to specialised skills, education and training. There is provision in law for an employer in an area of economic deprivation or decline to opt out, although it is seldom exercised.

Finally, there is the possibility for wage bargaining at the enterprise level; however, this is uncommon and, according to the OECD, only 0.01 percent of firms have company level agreements.

The process provides little leeway for differentiation of wages according to output or productivity. Such incentives are common only at management level.

Though salaries are low, the overall cost of remuneration is expensive. By tradition workers are paid 14 salaries - an extra month at Christmas and two weeks each at Easter and before their summer holiday. Leave entitlements are generous.

Social security contributions are paid on the full 14 salaries and can add half again to the cost of wages. The average outlay is equal to 44.06 percent of gross earnings - 28.06 percent employer and 16 percent employee. This covers basic pension and health care, supplementary pensions and other benefits such as unemployment insurance, widow's benefit etc.[12] Industrial employers pay an additional 1 percent because of the risk to their employees of accidents and occupational diseases.

Those engaged in 'onerous of arduous' may pay increased contributions that allow them to take their pensions five years ahead of mandatory retirement age. These can increase the total contribution to 50.66 percent - 31.21 percent employers and 19.45 percent employee. (Through collective bargaining agreements, 157 categories of workers have come to qualify for such benefits. According to the OECD the list includes as well as miners and asbestos workers, cheese and salami makers; bakery employees; persons involved in the production of make-

---

[12] Contributions are capped according to a formula that relates to the minimum wage that applied in 1993, GDP growth and certain other factors. The cap for entrants into the pension system before January 1, 2003 (when the contribution system was revamped) is approximately half that for those who entered the system subsequently - in 2006 €2,226 compared with €5,076.51. The self-employed pay lump sum contributions to the Free Professionals' Social Insurance Organisation (OAEE) according to a formula relating to the number of years the person has been insured.

up, medication and perfume; and *presenters of state-run television channels*.)

Table 17. Average social security contributions

(percent of gross earnings)

	Employer	Employee	Total
Social Insurance Institute (IKA)[a]	18.43	9.22	26.65
Supplementary Social Insurance Fund (ETEAM)[b]	3.00	3.00	6.00
Funds for other benefits	6.63	3.78	10.41
Total	28.06	16.00	44.06
Heavy work	*31.21*	*19.45*	*50.66*

[a]The social insurance fund for private sector employees. There are other funds for civil servants, military personnel, the self-employed, farmers, merchant seamen etc. A number of public enterprises have unique funds that are supposed to be merged with IKA by 2008. [b]The auxiliary insurance fund for IKA. There are an estimated 170 primary and auxiliary funds in Greece.

Source: *Taxing Wages: 2005/2006*, OECD, 2007

A major factor contributing to a lack of employee mobility is that redundancy payments are high - particularly for salaried personnel. Severance pay for blue-collar workers ranges from five days of pay for one year of service up to 160 days for 30 years. For white-collar workers, including executives, the redundancy rate is one month of salary for service up to one year gradually escalating to 24 months for 28 years.[13]

New Democracy has made overtures towards labour law reform, but in the main has focussed on improved management of the existing system rather than root-and-branch reform.

It repealed the Pasok overtime rates and restored those that had gone before so that employers now pay 125 percent of basic pay for the first five hours and 150 percent for the remaining three of the maximum eight allowable.[14]

In a measure designed both to promote competition and to increase the availability of part-time jobs, retail outlets have been allowed to stay

---

[13] *Employers are obliged to give notice of between five and 60 days for blue-collar workers and between 10 and 120 for white-collar, depending upon length of service.*

[14] *Law 3385/05. To provide for flexibility of staffing in seasonal industries, employers can request their employees to work a 10-hour day provided time- off is given in lieu and employees have the right to refuse without jeopardising their jobs. Such hours may also be invoked in smaller companies employing fewer than 20 people, provided the workforce concurs: previously, management had to secure the approval of the relevant sectoral associations or trade union federations.*

open until 9pm on weekdays and 8pm on Saturdays. Sunday opening remains banned.

According to official statistics, Greece ranks fourth from the bottom of the list of the 30 members of the OECD in terms of the proportion of the labour force that works part-time - just 5.8 percent of total employment compared with the average of 15 percent.[15]

The figures overlook the fact that in many sectors of the economy people hold several jobs in order to make ends meet. Where one would ordinarily expect a full-time employee to do an eight-hour shift, many Greeks hold two or more 'full-time' jobs based on five-hour shifts, of which they frequently perform as little as three.[16]

An issue that ND promised to tackle before it was elected but with which it has yet fully to get to grips is the number of persons in the public sector, working on temporary contracts. These are supposed to be fixed-term or seasonal and to allow short-term employment of extra workers to supplement staff complements stipulated by law that the state tries to minimise for reasons of economy.

Such arrangements have, however, become a vestibule to permanent employment with large numbers of persons prepared to work on temporary contracts for long periods - sometimes years - in anticipation of eventually securing public sector tenure. The situation has been the cause of many strikes under ND by workers seeking to transfer from contract to payroll status.

In the broader public sector, the government has sought to end the extension to the employees of public enterprises and entities the job security enjoyed by civil servants.

The DEKO law (*see page 81*) required that all new hires be made according to terms applying in the private sector and allowed that, if a public company was posting losses, management could change its personnel regulations to eliminate special clauses preventing layoffs.

The vanguard project was a voluntary retirement scheme agreed between the ND-appointed management at the Hellenic

---

[15] *According to the ESYE analysis of its statistics, 43.6 percent of part-timers only work part-time because they cannot find a full-time job, while 11.6 percent work part-time because they are also caring for children or incapacitated adults.*

[16] *Public servants are among those who most commonly hold a second job. Because they are forbidden to take outside employment, they are not able to declare the income earned from such work and thus are a major contributing factor to the unrecorded economy and its consequent tax loss to the state.*

Telecommunications Organisation (OTE) and the company union, OME-OTE, in June 2005. Under its terms, all workers over 50 were offered a highly generous redundancy package including a leaving bonus, full salary to retirement age and full pension rights. For some workers this meant golden handshakes equivalent to as much as €250,000.

Management proposed to replace a portion of these workers with younger personnel hired under private law contracts who would be both cheaper (because of their lack of seniority) and more useful (because of their higher degree of computer literacy).

A total of 5,562 applications were received – just over a third of OTE's workforce - of which the company accepted 4,759 at a cost of approximately €1bn.[17] Management expected to recoup the entire cost by the end of 2007 through savings in wages and pensions.

In 2006, OTE recruited 1,230 new employees,[18] 915 of them in engineering and technical positions.[19] For 2007-09, the company has fixed an annual limit on new hires of 50 and says that positions requiring new skills will be filled by retraining existing staff at the levels of both labour force and middle management.

OTE, which posted a loss in 2005 because of the voluntary redundancy scheme, sought to use the DEKO bill to change the tenure conditions of all its workforce. This could not be negotiated and the government had to legislate.[20] The *quid pro quo* for permitting easier layoffs was to introduce more flexible recruitment procedures allowing higher salaries and benefits for experienced and specialised personnel both at entry levels and in managerial positions.

The government claimed that the situation at OTE would become the new

---

[17] *Under Law 3371/05, the legislation which confirmed the arrangements, the state was to contribute 4 percent of its then 38.7 percent shareholding in OTE to TAP-OTE, the company's primary pension fund, to help offset the loss of contributions caused by so many redundancies. The Commission competition authorities allowed this to be done subject to a cap of €390.3m being put on the state's contribution. As of May 31, 2007, the share price on the Athens Stock Exchange valued 4 percent at €464.6m. In the section on risk factors in its annual 20-F filing to the US Securities and Exchange Commission on June 28, 2007, the OTE management commented (p 15): "We cannot, however, give you any assurance that the Greek state will perform this obligation to TAP-OTE to the full extent in accordance with the provisions of the relevant law." (*6)*

[18] *Overall, the exercise reduced the average of OTE employees to 44.25 years and the average number of years in service to 19.31.*

[19] *Overall staff numbers declined from 16,302 on December 31, 2004 to 11,775 on December 31, 2006, a net reduction of 27.8 percent.*

[20] *Law 3522/06.*

paradigm for employment in all public enterprises, but the intensity of the reaction in the trade union movement provoked by having to legislate the new employment terms caused it to get cold feet and, despite the fact that other major enterprises - such as the Public Power Corporation (DEI), the Hellenic Railways Organisation (OSE) and Olympic Airlines - would be prime candidates for comparable treatment, no further such action has been taken.[21]

To reduce the number of people without jobs, the government in 2004 introduced a National Action Plan for Employment[22] that provided stepped-up personalised counselling of the unemployed and efforts to improve job matching and skills by the Manpower Employment Organisation (OAED).[23]

It also provides employment subsidies for new entrants to the labour market, persons who have registered as looking for work but who have not yet been able to find a job. OAED pays employers an amount equivalent to their unemployment contributions, provided that the firm pays at least the national minimum wage and provides full insurance cover and does not lay off workers to make places for the subsidised employees.

Other measures include full subsidy of employers' social security contributions if they hire individuals who are parents of at least two children; 50 percent reductions in employers' social insurance contributions for new-hires under 25 or over 55; and subsidy of the social security contributions of temporary contract workers hired to replace women on maternity leave.

A second piece of legislation[24] provides for 'social' work in the form of fixed-term contracts of part-time employment for unemployed women, persons with more than three children, the longterm unemployed and persons close to the age of retirement to deal with people with special needs. Some 6,600 persons have been given jobs looking after some 50,000 people working in day care centres, children's play centres and community care units for the elderly.[25]

---

[21] When the board of directors of DEI offered lump sum payments of 20 months' wages to employees prepared to take voluntary redundancy in 2006, just 139 of the company's 26,800 personnel took advantage of the scheme.

[22] Law 3327/04.

[23] OAED has created computerised profiles of all unemployed persons with a view to matching them with job vacancies.

[24] Law 3250/04.

[25] For more details of the measures under Laws 3227/04 and 3250/04, see Greece, OECD Economic Surveys, Vol 2005/12, September 2005, pp 102-118.

To promote worker mobility, the government has provided a rent subsidy for unemployed persons prepared to take work away from their home towns[26] and offers through OAED housing assistance to people prepared to start their own business outside large urban centres.

That said, the OECD notes that Greek efforts in promoting active labour market programmes (ALMPs) have been weak with spending, relative to GDP (unrevised), less than one-third the eurozone average.

Under the umbrella of the revised Lisbon Strategy, the EU has been pressing member states to introduce policies promoting *flexi-security*: flexibility in employment legislation coupled with programmes of training, re-training and lifelong learning, designed to ensure rapid re-employment and thus remove the fear of dismissal.

The ND government's response has been positive - it has set itself the target of creating 400,000 new jobs by 2010 in order to bring the employment ratio to 64.1 percent - but its programme implementation has been slow. Legislation has been adopted[27] to promote lifelong learning, including the establishment of special education institutes at universities and technical colleges, but most practical programmes are still in the process of evolution for incorporation in the funding regime of the National Strategic Reference Framework (ESPA).

The *Implementation Report 2006 for the National Reform Programme* details the proposals at length[28] but, for the time being, practical measures consist of the formation of committees, the development of studies and the drafting of joint ministerial decisions to chart the way forward. One concrete development has been the use of CSF III funding to create 4,500 'all-day' schools and 2,000 kindergartens with a view to facilitating the employability of women.

The OECD in its 2007 report on Greece argued the need for immediate practical measures to differentiate labour costs and to facilitate market entry. For example, it suggested that instead of extending the National Minimum Wage Agreement to all private sector employees, its terms should apply only to those workers who are

---

[26] *Additionally, as from 2005, rents are deductible from income tax for persons under the age of 40 who move to take employment outside Athens or Thessaloniki and for any employee who is transferred outside his or her home town.*

[27] *Law 3369/05.*

[28] *See* National Reform Programme 2005-2008, Implementation Report 2006, *Ministry of Economy and Finance, October 2006, www.mnec.gr, pp 43-50.*

members of the unions participating in the negotiations.

This would require decentralised collective bargaining for remaining employees at the occupational and corporate level and could lead to linkage of their pay scales to their output.

To promote employment of unskilled young workers, the OECD argued there should be a sub-minimum entry-level wage for school leavers and other new market entrants that would reflect the amount employers would have to spend in training these youths in the tasks for which they are hired.[29]

The OECD argued that rather than enforcing uniform wages there should be a much more flexible scale with targeted social security benefits to compensate the least well-off. It recommended reduction of the social security contributions of the lowest paid in order to improve their level of take-home pay.

The report suggested that the difference in the rates of severance pay for blue- and white-collar workers should be rationalised. It said that Greece would do well to consider a severance programme introduced in Austria that has been designed to facilitate job mobility.

Under this scheme employers contribute 1.5 percent of each employee's payroll to an individualised account. If the employee quits or is fired within three years of taking a job, the pot is carried forward to the next employer; if he or she leaves after three years, the pot may be taken as severance pay or saved towards the creation of a future pension. The payments, known as the separation allowance, can be cumulated over an employee's entire working life.

The OECD argues that the system smoothes dismissal costs for employers and eliminates uncertainties related to redundancy payments for employees. Employers frequently reduce wage levels modestly to offset the extra cost. The report argues, however, that employees are more than compensated by the security afforded towards job mobility which is in line with the Lisbon concept of flexi-security.

---

[29] According to the OECD report, 21 of its 30 member states set a minimum wage of which 13 provide for a sub-minimum rate for youths or apprentices.

Education

THE ND government came to office pledging to spend 5 percent of GDP a year on education. But the ministry of national education and religious affairs (Ypepth) never managed more than 3.7 percent, compared with an average of 5.2 percent in the EU.[1]

Greece spends close to the average in the EU25 on primary education and a little above on tertiary[2] but lags well behind in spending on secondary at 1.39 percent of GDP, compared with the EU's 2.4 percent.[3]

When Greek performance is compared with that of the 30 nations of the OECD - including countries with a focus on education such as Canada, Australia, New Zealand and Japan - the country stands well down in the league tables. Spending per student is around $4,700, compared with an OECD average of $7,470 (ranking Greece 20th out of 30), while public expenditure on education as a percentage of total public expenditure is approximately 8 percent compared with 13.3 percent (which ranks Greece last).[4]

There is approximately one computer for every eleven 15-year-old pupils, ranking Greece number 22 out of 31 nations,[5] and on the OECD's PISA[6] scale of assessment of "mathematical literacy" Greece ranks third from last - just ahead of Turkey and Mexico.[7]

Enrolments in tertiary education have doubled in the past decade and graduation levels have been increasing but the level of dropouts, particularly from technical education colleges, is extremely high.[8] The

---

[1] In 2005, the expenditure constituted 3.62 percent of budget outlays; in 2006, 3.67 percent; and, for 2007, the projection is 3.1 percent.

[2] The respective figures for the EU25 are 1.15 percent of GDP and 1.14 percent.

[3] Third Competitiveness Report of the National Council for Competitiveness and Development (ESAA), Special Secretariat for Competitiveness, Ministry of Development, June 2006.

[4] Education at a Glance 2006, OECD, 2006.

[5] The OECD30 plus the Russian Federation.

[6] Programme for International Student Assessment.

[7] In Greece at least a quarter of all students fail to reach Pisa's Level Two of mathematical proficiency, which is defined as the level at which students "can use direct inference to recognise the mathematical elements of a situation, are able to use a single representation to help explore and understand a situation, can use basic algorithms, formulae and procedures and can make literal interpretations and apply direct reasoning". Other countries with similar deficiencies are Italy, Mexico, Portugal and Turkey. The proportion of Greek pupils reaching the highest levels of proficiency (five and six) is less than 6 percent.

[8] The dropout rates in esteemed Tertiary A courses - such as medicine, law and architecture - are well below the OECD average. However, for Tertiary B courses in more practical or technical subjects it reportedly is as high as two out of three, by far the highest.

percentage of students that travel abroad to study is approximately 8 percent, roughly double the OECD average.[9]

The Greek constitution (Article 16) provides that tertiary education is the responsibility of the state. There are 23 universities (AEI)[10] catering to around 210,000 students and 16 technological institutes (TEIs) providing places for some 170,000.[11] The duration of most undergraduate courses is four years, though for engineering, architecture and agriculture it is five and for medicine it is six.

Master's programmes do not form part of the Greek system but higher studies are available in more than 200 fields and offer a Postgraduate Diploma of Specialisation. The courses are at least one year long, more often two. Some universities do not offer postgraduate studies, but a student may proceed directly to the doctoral level after having met certain prerequisites. Doctoral studies are open-ended but three years is considered normal.

The fundamental problem of Greek higher education is that it has emphasised quantity over quality. To secure a tertiary education place, secondary students must sit exams that are marked out of 20.[12] Reportedly, it takes a score of at least 19 to obtain one of the much sought-after places in the top Athens or Thessaloniki faculties such as medicine, economics or law.

However, some students have been able to obtain places in technical colleges with results as low as 2/20. That said, some of the schools to which they have gained entry have been of a comparable standard. The classic horror story is the TEI that offered a course in hotel catering that taught cooking from the blackboard because there were no stoves in the school's kitchen-laboratory.

Students nominate their preferred schools but the ministry of education has the final say in who goes where and frequently allocates more pupils than the tertiary institutions feel they can handle.

---

[9] Greece has the second highest number of tertiary education students abroad after Ireland from where many students travel to schools nearby in the UK.

[10] Including the Open University based in Patra which has functioned since 1992 and the new Hellenic International University based in Thessaloniki scheduled to operate from September 2007.

[11] Additionally, there are higher education institutes providing training for teachers, priests, policemen, military officers, merchant seamen, artists, dancers, actors, practitioners of the fine arts and tourism professionals.

[12] There are also orals that account for 30 percent of the grading.

For 2005-06, the ND government said that in order to secure a place, a student would have to score a minimum of 10 points, which meant that 18,768 places, mostly in regional TEIs, went unfilled.

Ironically, there was a strong lobby from provincial communities where the schools were sited demanding that the criterion be rescinded since they had come to rely on the students to sustain their local economies.

For the 2007-08 schoolyear - an election year - the ministry is offering 36,685 new university places when the universities have said that they can only accommodate 25,132.[13]

Generally, the academic credentials of faculty are high but, as they are state employees, they have the same status and salary scales as civil servants.[14] There is no differentiation in salaries related to academic qualifications or publications and, therefore, no incentive to do any more than the minimum of teaching or research.

Professors are notorious for not turning up to class, leaving lecturing to their juniors, while they supplement their salaries by sitting on expert committees or doing consulting work for ministerial departments and public enterprises.

Conversely, many of those registered as students are simply time-servers, escaping the military draft or engaged in political activism. The OECD estimates that less than 70 percent of those registered as students actually study, while only around 30 percent attend classes.

Students may resit their exams as often as they like and, as of the end of the 2005-06 academic year, there were an estimated 94,000 undergraduates who had been attending classes for eight years or more[15] leading to a phenomenon known as "the perpetual student". The government's rationale for not having met its education-spending commitments is that there is no point in throwing good money after bad until the system is reformed.

To consider measures for change, the government created the National Council for Education (ESYP), a forum for 38 interest groups, under the chairmanship of Thanos Veremis, a distinguished professor

---

[13] "Tertiary education reform bill approved in the face of violent protests", Greek Economics BiWeekly, Eurobank EFG, March 13, 2007.

[14] Administrators are also public officials.

[15] "Parliament battle against bill", Athens News, March 2, 2007.

of political science. After prolonged debate, boycotted by a number of the groups, ESYP's ideas were passed to a committee of eight 'wise men' who hammered them into a blueprint for legislative change. In May 2006, it proposed, among other things, that

- students should have half again the official time to complete their studies (eg, six years for a four-year course) or be asked to stand down;[16]

- academics should provide a written report at the end of each semester about their teaching over the previous six months and these should be used by university authorities to assess their role; and

- the rector's office should be relieved of administrative duties and these should be assigned either to academics trained in business management or to experts in administration with full responsibility for university finances.[17]

Another suggestion was to end the practice of having the state finance one textbook per course (usually the professor's) and to introduce reading lists coupled with increased spending on library resources and improved access to publications by means of the Internet.

The government said it welcomed the proposals and immediately brought forward draft legislation, but this prompted bitter reaction from both students and professors. The students occupied campuses and took to the streets in repeated violent demonstrations, while teachers, members of the Panhellenic Federation of University Faculty Associations (POSDEP), staged a prolonged strike.[18]

The government withdrew two drafts of the legislation for further consultation, primarily in hopes of keeping Pasok on board in a parallel exercise to amend the constitution in order to allow the establishment of private universities (*see page 115*).

When the socialists definitively refused to cooperate in the constitutional amendment process, the government in early March 2007 pushed its much watered-down reforms through parliament without further change.

---

[16] *Three examiners, excluding the course professor, would decide the fate of a student who fails to pass his final semester exams in any course three times.*

[17] *For further details see, "University overhaul on track", Athens News, May 5, 2006.*

[18] *For many weeks, members of staff who were not members of POSDEP felt they could not break the strike, though ultimately they disregarded it and returned to work in defiance of their colleagues' action.*

Under the new law[19]

- students must take their degrees within twice the allotted course time (eg, eight years for a four-year course) or leave without them;

- tertiary educational establishments must draw up four-year business plans which will form the basis for state allocations of funds; and

- secretaries must be appointed on four-year contracts to coordinate financial and administrative services under the supervision of the rector; the secretary will have particular responsibility for the implementation of decisions relating to assessment and quality assurance (*see page 113*);

From 2008, tertiary educational institutions are to have greater autonomy in decisions over how many students they will be required to accept each year.

The legislation dropped provisions for improved assessment of staff performance by means of peer review.

Representation and asylum

Two non-academic issues were the cause of much of the contention over the education reforms.

The first involved the role of students in university decision-making. Since shortly after Pasok first acceded to power in the early 1980s, students have had a role in electing rectors and deciding other issues related to university governance.[a]

Their vote, however, has been exercised through their student union representatives, who are politicised along party lines and frequently drawn from among the ranks of the "the perpetual students".

The amendments say that henceforth students should cast their vote directly in balloting for the rector, a proposal which was fiercely opposed by the student activists.

The other issue concerned university asylum. Security authorities have not had the right to enter a university campus (except to pursue crimes of violence against the person such as murder or rape) unless invited by the university authorities in the shape of the Rector's Council. This right was designed to guarantee that individuals could not be prosecuted for their expression of ideas.

Asylum became a politically sensitive issue after it was violated by the colonels' dictatorship in 1973 when the army stormed the Athens

---

[19] *Law 3549/07.*

Polytechnic to end an anti-junta occupation. Scores of students and bystanders died and hundreds were injured.

Latterly, however, university asylum has been abused by criminals (such as drug dealers) and anarchists who, having committed criminal acts, have then fled to the sanctuary of the campus to escape arrest.

To invite the police to enter the campus required a unanimous decision of the Rector's Council, which gave the student representative an effective right of veto.

The revisions provided for majority voting - thus finessing that veto - and only recognised asylum in cases relating to academic freedom. The proviso has been renamed "academic" as opposed to "university" asylum.

^aUniversity Law 1268/1982 and TEI Law 1404/1983.

The European Union - as part of the Bologna Process (designed to support the Lisbon Process) - is seeking to institute a European standard for tertiary education by 2010 with an agreed programme known as 3+2: a three-year undergraduate degree coupled with a two-year postgrad qualification. The programme seeks to implement quality standards that will allow academic credits and diplomas from one country automatically to be recognised in the others. The process even pursues joint degrees awarded through universities in two different member states. Directives have been issued requiring evaluation of study programmes, assessment of quality standards and mutual recognition of degrees.

The ND government reforms approximate the EU standards but, because of reluctance to change on the part of politicians and resistance on the part of students and staff, do not fulfil them in all cases. There is a risk that Greek degrees will not prove acceptable in other EU countries after the end of this decade.

To ensure continent-wide standards, the Bologna Process set European Guidelines and Standards to cover national quality-assurance programmes. The ND government created the Hellenic Quality Assurance Agency (ADIP)[20] consisting of 15 representatives of AEIs, TEIs, students, researchers and external chambers responsible for technical disciplines. It was slated to begin to function in 2007.

Every four years, universities will undertake self-assessments that will involve students as well as teaching/research, scientific and administrative staff. These will be evaluated by a five-man external evaluation committee, which will also make on-site visits to interview staff and students.

The evaluations will be put to ADIP, which will review the findings and compile a report for parliament. The agency will keep a database available for public consultation. Plans call eventually for an education ombudsman.

If the debate that preceded the establishment of this system is anything to go by, these assessments will represent the lowest common denominator of the cumulative interests of all the groups involved. They will be descriptive and not prescriptive and there will be no penalties for poor performance - a point stressed by the minister in order to get the schools and students to accept even the notion of evaluation.

Some commentators have argued that they should form the basis for the allocation of funding of educational establishments. This notion has been dismissed by the authorities because already the better performing universities are the ones that are best funded.

Greek law permits the transfer of credits from other European universities to the Greek system and foresees the possibility of dual doctoral studies at a Greek and an EU university leading to the award of a joint PhD.

However, the recognition of purely foreign degrees for employment in Greece remains highly contentious. Historically, the authorities - pressed by local academic and professional bodies - refused to recognise the degrees of all but the most prestigious foreign universities, particularly in technical fields such as medicine and engineering.

The Inter-University Centre for the Recognition of Foreign Degrees (DIKATSA) was noted for its prolonged deliberations (months and sometimes years) and arbitrary decisions. There were constant arguments over different standards, particularly in technical disciplines where local associations and chambers sought to sustain their domestic closed shops.

The ND government, seeking to comply with EU rules on mutual recognition, abolished DIKATSA and in 2005 replaced it with the National Agency for the Recognition of Foreign Degrees (DOATAP). This was supposed to be staffed by specialists familiar with foreign academic standards working on three-year contracts so that they did not become an entrenched part of the system and thus subject to its internal pressures.

A wider range of degrees is now recognised, but the agency can demand extensive, hard-to-obtain details about the background to degrees that it would rather not acknowledge.

Article 16 of the constitution declares tertiary education to be preserve of the state and stipulates that it should be offered for free.[21]

It is possible to set up a company that charges fees to teach tertiary level skills. These are registered by Ypepth as institutions of learning but are refused the title of AEI or TEI and must refer to themselves as Centres of Liberal Studies (KES).[22] The KES are controlled by the Commerce Secretariat of the Ministry of Development, as though they were retail service companies.

There are 37 KES in Greece providing training in everything from optometry to business administration. Standards are mixed but some hold franchises from foreign universities and have obtained international certification from agencies - such as the British Accreditation Council for Further and Higher Education - that have assessment standards higher than those that apply to Greek, state-sector, tertiary establishments.

Successive Greek governments have refused nonetheless to recognise the KES degrees as valid for the purposes of employment in the public sector.

Under EU rules, the diplomas of franchise-holding KES ought to be recognised as three-year undergraduate qualifications under the European 3+2 model. Greece had until October 2007 to implement the latest directive[23] modernising the recognition rules.

The government continued to fight a rearguard action, citing the principle of subsidiarity, although it has hinted that it might be prepared to compromise in cases where the universities awarding the franchises can demonstrate that they are active in both the establishment and monitoring of the quality standards in the local schools using their name.

In March 2007 (within days of passing its tertiary education reform bill), the government passed through parliament 49 proposals for constitutional amendments,[24] among them one amending Article 16 so as to allow the establishment of fee-paying, not-for-profit universities.

To amend the constitution requires that a proposal be passed by one

---

[21] There are no fees for undergraduate and doctoral students, though there are some charges for students pursuing postgraduate specialist studies.

[22] Article 16, paragraph 8 of the constitution provides that "the establishment of university-level institutions by private persons is prohibited".

[23] 2005/36/EU.

[24] Forty-three of its own and six advanced by Pasok.

parliament and endorsed by the next. The procedure requires that a proposal be passed in the current parliament by a three-fifths majority (180 votes) after which it can be passed in the next by a simple majority; or vice versa.

Initially, the socialist leader, George Papandreou, implied that Pasok would support amendment of Article 16 but, because free higher education is part of the socialist credo of many Pasok backbenchers and because the establishment of not-for-profit universities had become confused in the mind of the electorate with ND's tertiary reform legislation, Pasok walked out of parliament when the issue came to a vote.

This means that ND has only a simple majority for its proposed amendment and must find allies to make up the majority to three-fifths majority in the next parliament - always assuming it wins the election. On present evidence it is unlikely that it will be able to secure the necessary number of votes so it will be 2012 before such a reform can be brought forward again and sometime after 2016 before it could be implemented.

The OECD in its 2007 report on the Greek economy described the government's education reforms as a step in the right direction but said they were "modest as compared to the scale of the deficiencies identified..."[25]

It called for greater focus on the evaluation of universities and linkage of their funding to the findings about their performance. For this to happen, though, there would have to be an end to centralised decision-making - particularly in the assignment of students.

As George Babiniotis, rector of Athens University, has been quoted as saying, "You can't assess me if I've planned to put 100 students in a certain department and the state forces me to take 250."[26]

The OECD suggests that more rigorous initial selection of students would prevent wastage of resources on the large proportion who drop out.

Even then, it noted that Greek public funding levels are so low that consideration should be given to topping them up with the introduction

[25] Greece, *OECD Economic Surveys, Volume 2007/5, May 2007, p 110.*
[26] *"Babiniotis draws a gun on Yannakou",* Athens News, July 7, 2006.

of low-rate tuition fees for undergraduate students. Students who do not have the resources could be offered loans with payment contingent on them achieving a certain income threshold once they graduate and find work.[27]

The report argued that the introduction of fees would make students anxious to finish their studies more quickly. Moreover, it says, other OECD countries have found that the introduction of fees and income-contingent loan schemes have gone hand in with a "considerable" rise in rates of graduation. The government dismissed out of hand the notion of charging fees within the state system.

The OECD warmly endorsed the notion of allowing private universities. It said they would allow benchmarking in terms of standards and should be welcomed - rather than opposed - by academics since they would offer new career opportunities and "might inject some dynamism into research performance which is currently poor"[28] (*see inset on page 118*).

Continuing vocational training is not common in Greece. In 2004, just 20.5 percent of all employees were engaged in some sort of educational activity or training programme. This compared with an average of 48.8 percent in the EU25 and levels in excess of 80 percent in some countries (eg, Finland and Slovenia).[29]

This is particularly a problem for young people. Greece has the second highest ratio in the OECD30 of the working population aged between 25 and 29 that is not in education, employment or training (NEET). Only in Poland is the figure higher.[30] Moreover, in Greece some 20 percent of youths remain in the NEET category for up to five years.

The Greek system includes initial vocational education institutes (IEK) and Continuing Education Centres (KEK) that offer accreditation for the job market but not for further studies. These have been funded

---

[27] *The report acknowledged that the chaotic state of the Greek fiscal services would make monitoring this recommendation a difficult, if not impossible, task.*

[28] Greece, *OECD Economic Surveys, Volume 2007/5, May 2007, p 110.*

[29] Third Competitiveness Report of the ESAA, *June 2006, section 3.3.3. Education and skills. The council did not elaborate on the criteria behind these figures. The OECD put the proportion of the working population aged 25-64 participating in continuing education or training at 3.7 percent compared with an EU average of 10 percent. The government in its preliminary work on CSF IV (again the criteria are not defined) has targeted further education or training for 8 percent of the population aged 25-64 by 2013.*

[30] Education at a Glance, *OECD, 2006.*

in large measure through Community Support Framework programmes.

In the years immediately after their inception, they developed a reputation as vehicles to absorb funding rather than centres of quality training. Instructors, often trade unionists who had been made redundant from their jobs, taught outmoded skills on cast-off industrial equipment that had long been superseded in the workplace. The worst of these problems have been addressed but the centres still have a dubious reputation.

One of the targets of the government's National Reform Programme is to use funding from the ESPA so that every young person leaving school is offered either a) a job, b) an apprenticeship, c) additional training, or d) "[an]other employability measure in line with his individual needs".[31]

Ypepth has secured €3.3bn for continuing education programmes[32] - one-third of which is to be spent on infrastructure. For the time being, the programme is at the development stage with the authorities monitoring the magnitude of the problem that needs to be addressed. Ultimately, OAED will be called upon to create jobs, to provide grants for those wishing to start their own businesses and to devise training opportunities to promote career development.

The government has drafted legislation on lifelong learning[33] that provides for specialised institutes at universities and technical colleges with programmes coordinated by a standing Lifelong Learning Committee.

After many years getting off the ground, a new National System for Linking Vocational Education and Training with Employment (ESSEEKA) finally has begun to function, leading to hopes that training schemes in future will be more attuned to the actual needs of business.

R&D and innovation

Greece spent just 0.58 percent of GDP on research and development in 2004, compared with 1.9 percent in the EU25 (1.95 percent in the EU15).[a] The Lisbon Strategy calls for the EU level to rise to 3 percent by 2010; the National Reform Programme targets 1.5 percent in Greece.

---

[1] National Reform Programme 2005-2008, *p 44.*

[2] *"Gov't plan for lifelong learning",* Kathimerini (English edition), *June 28, 2007.*

[3] *Law 3369/05*

The number of young people aged 25-34 with doctorates in the fields of science and technology is roughly one-third the EU average and the percentage of researchers in the total population is about 70 percent that in the EU.

Whereas in the EU the funding ratio for R&D is approximately 1:1 public:private, in Greece it is 3:2, with most of the private funding concentrated in a very small number of businesses.

Companies claim that they farm out a lot of their R&D on contract to universities and other research centres but, according to the National Council for Competitiveness and Development (ESAA), "total spending is so low that one cannot defend the view that businesses are underperforming because they assign their R&D to the universities instead of conducting in-house research".[b]

One of the problems is that many of the largest and most successful Greek manufacturing firms with products having significant technological input work to foreign designs acquired under licence through royalty agreements.

The result is reflected in the number of patents applied for from Greece. The volume of applications filed with the European Patent Office is around eight per million of population per year compared with 133 for the EU25 (and no fewer than 311 in Finland). Only Portugal performs more poorly than Greece.

When applications to the US Patent and Trademark Office are considered, Greece fares even worse, with a rate of two per million compared with 60 in the EU25 (158 for Finland).

[a]*Third Competitiveness Report of the ESAA,* Special Secretariat for Competitiveness, Ministry of Development, June 2006, section 3.3.4. [b]*Ibid.*

Liberalisation

ACCORDING to UNCTAD's annual survey of national potential to attract foreign direct investment (FDI), Greece ranks fractionally outside the top quarter of the 141 countries surveyed. When actual inflows are measured, however, it ranks in the bottom 15 percent (*see page 38*).

Economic fundamentals are favourable: GDP growth is strong, the currency is stable, inflation is slightly higher than the eurozone norm but low in relation to other countries of the region. Labour is no longer cheap but the calibre of the workforce compensates. The country is not in the economic heartland of Europe but it is an important locus for the Balkans, the broader region of Southeast Europe and the Middle East.[1] These factors combined should make Greece a focus for development investment.

The stumbling block has been the refusal of successive governments to allow market forces to prevail. Instead, most business activity is subject to extensive legislation, regulation or direct state control.

The OECD in a 2005 study[2] calculated that improvements in the regulation of Greek markets would produce one-off and ongoing gains in multi-factor productivity (MFP) - the combined productivity of labour and capital - that would increase output by up to 3.6 percent.[3]

In its 2007 economic overview, it argued that an easing of product market regulations could result in an increase in the Greek FDI to GDP ratio of around 80 percent. It is currently 13.2 percent. This, in turn, the OECD said, could increase the average employment rate by 1.5 to two percentage points (currently 59.3 percent).

With the exception of the New Democracy administration under Constantine Mitsotakis (1990-93), all Greek governments of the post-dictatorship era - regardless of political persuasion - have been statist by nature.[4]

---

[1] *Particularly in terms of financial services and telecoms and energy inter-connections.*

[2] The benefits of liberalising product markets and reducing barriers to international trade and investment: the case of the United States and the European Union, *Working Paper (2005)19, OECD, May 26, 2005.*

[3] *There has obviously been improvement in the course of the past decade as a 1998 study had said that liberalisation of product markets would increase output between five and seven percentage points.* See Robert McDonald, The Competitiveness of the Greek Economy 2005, *Athens News [Books], 2005, pp 127-128.*

[4] Ibid, *pp 111-124.*

Pasok governments under Costas Simitis recognised the need for privatisation to raise funds to contain debt as part of the convergence process to secure entry into the EMU, but their tactics targeted revenue raising and not cession of state control. Public enterprises were part-privatised through listing on the stock exchange; however, in every instance (apart from the banking sector), the government retained a blocking minority interest sufficient to continue to exercise strategic control.

New Democracy in opposition under Costas Karamanlis said that it would divest public enterprises so that market forces might prevail while ensuring orderly operation through the provision of strong regulators. In government, however, it has pursued only a limited privatisation programme.

To comply with EU rules, it granted virtual autonomy to the telecoms regulator, the National Telecommunications and Post Commission (EETT). But it abolished the Coastal Maritime Transport Authority (RATHE), dividing its competences between the Ministry of Merchant Marine and the Competition Committee, and it retained the advisory role assigned under Pasok legislation to the Regulatory Authority for Energy (RAE).[5]

The European Union, as part of its efforts to create an integrated single market, has been pressing member states to liberalise network industries in transport, telecoms, and energy. Greek governments have very reluctantly complied, usually late and often only under the threat of prosecution by the European Commission for failing to transpose and implement directives. The requisite domestic legislation satisfies the letter of EU law, but the spirit in which it is applied continues to favour the public over the private sector.

The result is that there is significant foreign investment waiting in the wings to enter the Greek market - particularly in the energy sector - but specific projects continue on hold while the investors' Greek partners seek ways to come to terms with, or to circumvent, the dead hand of the Greek state.

---

[5] It drafts legislation and codes and offers opinions on the applications of new market entrants but the final law texts and licences are the responsibility of the Minister of Development. RAE does have the final say on certain technical matters regarding the electricity grid and the natural gas pipeline network.

Transport and communications

Road

The independent road haulage sector is small, with the number of third-party vehicles estimated at around 5 percent of the total fleet. Independents - including owner-operators and small cartage firms - have managed over the years to persuade successive ministers to limit the number of licences, arguing the need to sustain incumbents' income.

The number of permits is fixed by ministerial decision according to an assessment of national and international needs. In 2005, eg, no new third-party licences were granted. As a consequence, most businesses maintain their own fleets at considerable cost in both vehicles and staff. Greater ability to outsource would decrease overheads significantly.

Transport tariffs used to be divided into three basic categories: short-haul (within a prefecture), medium-haul (across prefectural boundaries) and long-haul (international).

There were minimum and maximum rates in each category, with the levels kept high on medium- and long-haul routes to compensate drivers for having to deadhead home.

EU rules allowing foreign long-haul carriers to pick up cargoes for return-leg journeys introduced competition on international routes. The need for owner-operators to compete with own-account carriers has meant that rates for intra-regional carriage have also been freed.

There still remain restrictions on rates charged by operators of vehicles of more than 3.5 tonnes that haul across regional boundaries, though liberalisation is under consideration.

Urban transport systems (buses, trolleys and the Metro) are owned by state corporations and their staff are public employees. Fares are strictly regulated, ostensibly on social grounds, though in large measure for political reasons. Politicians believe that, on balance, the favourable impression on the average citizen created by the immediacy of cheap fares is greater than the negative one arising from abstract considerations such as budget deficits and public debt.

The transport company losses have been contained of late because of the improvement of their fleets ahead of the Olympic Games.

Inter-urban buses and local taxis are private, though again the number of licences is restricted in exchange for the state being allowed to set fares. These are kept well below international rates, with the result that standards of maintenance and service generally are poor. Taxi drivers supplement their incomes by carrying multiple fares, a practice which is illegal but to which the authorities turn a blind eye.

Monitoring the finances of owner-operators for purposes of taxation is a headache for the authorities. The government has sought to have drivers join in cooperatives or companies which would introduce book-keeping that would facilitate collection. The companies would be given freedom to set fares; in exchange the award of licences would be freed.

Rail

To comply with EU directives, legislation has been passed to create an independent company to manage the rail network and to oversee third-party access.[6] The legislation was passed two years late and the presidential decree governing terms of access has still not been published. As a consequence, the Hellenic Railways Organisation (OSE) retains a monopoly over domestic transport of both passengers and freight.

In keeping with the legislation, two new companies have been carved out of OSE: Edisy[7], to manage the network, and Trenose, to operate the company's trains and buses. These were established in January 2006 but at the time of writing the allocation of assets and personnel was not yet complete.

The notion is that Trenose should operate according to commercial principles, with managerial and operational autonomy, including the right to set passenger fares and freight tariffs. Edisy, like track-operators in many other countries, will be subsidised by the state. OSE has become a holding company for these plus four other companies:

- Ergose, which manages development projects co-financed under CSF programmes;

- Proastiakos SA, which is responsible for the development of suburban commuter lines;

- Gaiaose, which is supposed to develop the company's significant real-estate holdings; and

- Logistics Centres, which is responsible for the development of a

---

[6] *Presidential Decree 41/2005:* Regarding the harmonization of the Greek legislation with Directives 2001/12/EC, 2001/13/EC, 2001/14/EC of 26 February 2001 on the development of community railways, the granting of licences to railway undertakings, the capacity allocation of railway infrastructures, the charge for the use of railway infrastructure and safety certification.

[7] *National Administrator of Railway Infrastructure.*

major marshalling yard plus warehousing and storage facilities on the Thriassio Plain, inland from Elefsina, that will provide a node for rail transshipment of container traffic to and from Piraeus, Patra and Thessaloniki.

OSE can plead Greece's mountainous terrain in mitigation of its delays in double-tracking and electrifying the network. It has also had to cope with the fact that the network consists of two different gauges of track. But the system is also deficient in modern signalling and telemetry, which has been a major factor in its poor safety record.

A scheme for a western network from Kalamata in the southwestern Peloponnese to Igoumenitsa[8] on the northwestern coast of the mainland (with a link to the eastern seaboard north-south link via Ioannina and Kalambaka) has been under study since 1992 but is still at the stage of spatial planning.

OSE is hugely overmanned and regularly posts large losses that are funded through subsidies from the budget and state-guaranteed borrowing. Aggregate debts are estimated to be of the order of €1.2bn.

Sea

'Blue water' shipping is totally open, the only barrier to entry being the funds necessary to finance a fleet, something that was relatively easy in the middle years of this decade given the high levels of international liquidity.

The Greek beneficially owned fleet is the largest in the world, standing in early 2007 at 3,699 vessels of 218.2m deadweight tonnes.[9] In 2006 it contributed €14.3bn[10] to the balance of payments - equivalent to 39.4 percent of the trade deficit, or 60.5 percent of the current account deficit.

Only 969 of the vessels (26 percent of the number but 32 percent by deadweight) flew the Greek flag because of conditions regarding manning levels that made the Greek registry uncompetitive with flags of convenience such as Liberia, Malta and Panama.

The Ministry of Merchant Marine (YEN) hopes to see the Greek-registered fleet rise to around 1,500 vessels following the introduction

---

[8] With a ferry link across the Gulf of Corinth.
[9] As of February 16. 2007. according to the annual survey prepared for the London-based Greek Shipping Cooperation Committee by Lloyd's Register-Fairplay.
[10] This is the Bank of Greece figure for transportation earnings that are primarily from shipping.

of measures in 2006 to reduce the required number of Greek officers and to subsidise the social insurance contributions of other mandatory Greek crew.

The coastal shipping sector remains under close supervision by the YEN. Greece had an 11-year derogation from EU rules that liberalised the ferry sector from 1993.[11] It was designed to allow Greek shipowners time to renew their fleets in order to be able to compete with large northern European ferry companies in the event they decided to operate in Greek waters.

The 2001 legislation introduced by the last Pasok government to 'liberalise' the sector[12] continued to apply such strictures on manning, operational routines, routes and fares that the European Commission in December 2005 commenced infringement proceedings.

The ND government maintained the Pasok legislation, arguing that controls were necessary to ensure adequate service for the populations of Greece's many islands off the popular tourist routes on which large ferry operators focus.

After prolonged negotiations between the government, the Commission and ferry companies, a regime has been devised whereby fares have been freed for sailings from Piraeus, provided that the routes have annual traffic of at least 150,000 and two operators or 300,000 if there is only one.[13]

The commission has allowed that the state should offer an extensive subsidy programme under public service orders to ensure adequate coverage of less travelled routes.[14] Brussels has not lifted the infringement proceedings but neither has it pursued them.

The New Democracy government has drafted a €6bn, 10-year programme (2006-15) to upgrade the infrastructure in the country's 12 national ports.[15] To this end it has negotiated a €3bn soft loan facility with the European Investment Bank, the intention being to leverage this through concession development. The concept faltered at the first hurdle.

---

[11] *Regulation 3577/92 which applied from January 1, 1993. The Greek derogation expired on January 1, 2004.*

[12] *Law 2932/01.*

[13] *The scheme applies to 27 long-haul and popular short-haul routes.*

[14] *For background, see Robert McDonald, "It can't be Christmas every day", Special Survey No 60, Business File, Kerkyra Publications, Athens, June 2006, pp 64-70.*

[15] *Alexandroupolis, Corfu, Elefsina, Igoumenitsa, Iraklio, Kavala, Lavrio, Patra, Piraeus, Rafina, Thessaloniki and Volos.*

In mid-November 2006, the ND-appointed management of the Piraeus Port Authority (OLP)[16] approved terms for expansion of its Neo Ikonio container port at Perama which currently has two piers (one small and one large) with annual throughput capacity of 1.6m TEUs.[17]

The proposal called for a private concessionaire to invest €500m in expansion of the smaller pier and the construction of a third to add 2m TEUs of capacity and to create 2,000 new jobs in exchange for a 30-year management contract.

The stevedores' union, led by fewer than 40 gantry-crane operators fearful of losing extensive overtime payments, staged a seven-week work-to-rule which cost OLP at least €12m (maybe more) and led to losses several times that amount for retailers who had consignments delayed during the key sales period before Christmas.

The YEN ultimately intervened to have OLP suspend the tender and invited the workforce to make alternative proposals. These were to have been forthcoming by Spring 2007 but nothing since has been heard of the project.

Prior to this, leading global operators - particularly China Ocean Shipping Company (COSCO) - had been queueing to participate in Greek port development. Now they are reported to have transferred their attentions to ports in Turkey, Italy and Spain.[18]

The unions have taken the blame for the disruption but there are those who claim that some senior staff of OLP (other than key ND-appointed executives) were not unhappy to see the privatisation of management thwarted.

Under UN anti-terrorism conventions, maritime states are supposed to be upgrading security installations at major cargo ports. The YEN has announced a €340m scheme of improvements for the national ports (*see Table 14*) to be developed under public-private-partnership arrangements. So far, there has been no word as to whether the unions might object to the private participation in this scheme.

---

[16] *OLP is listed on the Athens Stock Exchange but is still 74.15 percent state-owned.*

[17] *20-foot equivalent units, the international standard for containers which come in 20- and 40-foot lengths.*

[18] *On June 4, 2007, COSCO's deputy director, Ken Chan, was cited by Reuters as saying that the company was still "interested in participating in any port investment opportunities with regard to Greek ports". However, he added that trade activities "might be hindered by the challenge of insufficient infrastructure investment in the region".*

Air

In theory, the air industry in Greece is fully liberalised. All EU carriers have the right to pick up and put down within Greece and to fly services to third countries from Greek airports without interconnecting with a national base (eg, British Airways could fly routes directly between Thessaloniki and Milan if there were sufficient traffic to support it).

The Mitsotakis government ended the monopoly of state-owned Olympic Airways and issued new licences for both passenger and cargo carriers. But once Pasok resumed office, such preferential treatment was given to the national carrier that most of the private operators could not compete and the new firms either failed or were forced to merge until today the only significant alternative carrier is Aegean Airlines.[19]

Olympic, which has never turned a profit since being nationalised in 1975, has massive aggregate debts in excess of its capitalisation[20] and has only been kept alive through state subsidies, direct and indirect. Among various measures have been the non-remittance of airport tax (which the company was permitted to use for operational expenses),[21] non-payment of airport handling charges and deferment of staff social security contributions.

Since 1998, there have been five tenders to privatise the airline - all unsuccessful. As part of the preparations for the first three, Pasok governments provided the airline with €161m in state aid. This was approved by the European Commission competition authorities on the understanding that the company would be successfully divested. In December 2002, after the failure of the third tender, the commission ruled that the sum had to be reimbursed to budget coffers.

Olympic Airways did not have the money and should have been put into liquidation. The Pasok government, however, made a last-ditch effort to sell Olympic.

In December 2003, it carved out of Olympic Airways a new company,

---

[19] The airline which has a fleet of 25 (mostly Boeing 737s and 747s) claims a 50 percent market share of domestic traffic. In July 2007 it floated on the Athens Stock Exchange in an IPO that raised €136m, the bulk of which will go towards the financing of a fleet expansion programme. The company has nineteen A320s on order at a cost of $800m with options on a further eight.

[20] Estimates vary between €0.5bn and €1bn, depending on what is included in the total.

[21] The theory being that the government would have to provide such funding in any event.

Olympic Airlines, and consigned to it 1,800 of Olympic Airways' staff of 6,000; its fleet of 47 aircraft; and all the routes and slots of its three arms: Olympic Airways (international), Olympic Aviation (domestic) and Macedonian Airways (charter). The assets transferred were worth some €130m.

Olympic Airways continued to exist, carrying the historical burden of debt and the remaining staff with its income limited to that generated by its subsidiary companies that performed ground handling, maintenance, engineering, fuelling, catering and booking. These were to provide services to Olympic Airlines under contract and themselves be prepared for privatisation, the proceeds to be used to pay down Olympic Airways debts. The tender for the sale of this new entity was interrupted by the March 2004 elections.

In September that year the ND government launched a fifth tender and in August 2005 it signed a preliminary memorandum of understanding with a preferred bidder (Olympic Investors/York Capital) for a sum reported to be of the order of €130m[22] plus a comparable amount in restructuring investment.

The deal was suspended one month later after the European Commission took the Olympic case to the European Court of Justice and secured a ruling that not only had the government to reclaim from Olympic the €161m in privatisation aid, it also had to claw back a further €540m related to indirect assistance and the costs of restructuring Airways into Airlines.[23]

Rather than declare the company bankrupt, the government passed legislation to protect Olympic from its creditors while it embarked on yet another restructuring exercise.

It has now created a third incarnation known as Pantheon Airways,

---

[22] In its first two years of operation, the new airline managed to accumulate losses of €107m.

[23] "Commission finds that Greece has granted illegal state aid to Olympic Airways and Olympic Airlines", Press release, IP/05/1139, European Commission, September 14, 2005. The commission ruled that Olympic Airlines represented a legal continuum of Olympic Airways and was not a discrete entity. It itemised the new amounts to be reimbursed as €350m in unpaid tax and social security contributions accrued by Olympic Airways, the €130m in start-up assets consigned from Airways to Airlines and €60m in new debt obligations assumed by the state on behalf of Airways/Airlines. The commission asked the ECJ to impose retroactive fines on the Greek state of €10,512 a day for failure to comply with the 2002 ruling and recommended fines of €53,611 a day so long as the second lot of funds was not reclaimed. At the time of writing, the court's decision on these demands was pending.

capitalised at €60m, which it says it will privatise just as soon as it can resolve with the Brussels competition authorities the issue of the aid rebates. The sale, which was the responsibility of Petros Doukas, then deputy minister of economy and finance, has been cloaked in strict secrecy.

The latest wheeze, according to a press report,[24] is that the government is seeking to offset against the €540m, a sum of €580m which a Greek arbitration court has ordered the government to pay the airline as compensation for the cost of relocation of its operations base at the old Elliniko airport to the new Eleftherios Venizelos Airport.

If such an arrangement were approved by Brussels, it would in fact mean a fresh infusion of capital of the order of €40m, potentially making the airline more attractive to investors.[25] (*7)

A major issue in the effort to sell Olympic continues to be its bloated workforce. The company is massively overmanned with militant unions representing both air crew and ground staff. Neither Pasok governments nor the current ND administration has been prepared to pay the political cost of laying off so many people; indeed PM Karamanlis left his government a hostage to fortune when, during his 2005 annual state of the economy address in Thessaloniki, he promised that "none of Olympic's employees will be left out on the street". This implied that the government would provide alternative public sector employment for the company's hundreds of supernumeraries.

According to the press report about the netting of debt obligations, the government plans to negotiate with Olympic workers their participation in the privatisation sale, though whether this would be acceptable to new private managers remains to be seen.

The Greek state controls 55 percent of the joint venture that owns Athens International Airport. Hochtief, the German contractor which constructed the airport, holds the balance, together with private partners and has a 30-year operating concession until 2026.

Hochtief has incorporated part of its holding into a real-estate investment trust (REIT). The ND government at one point indicated that it intended to do the same, contributing 20 percentage points of its

---

[24] *"Ultimate plan for saving Olympic Airlines this fall"*, Kathimerini (English edition), *June 9, 2007.*
[25] *The government contends that, if the airline is ultimately sold, the reclaim of the €161m should not be necessary as it will have contributed to the company's privatisation.*

holding to a REIT that also would incorporate assets from Greek provincial airports and be floated on the Athens Stock Exchange.

The government was not, however, able to reach agreement with Hochtief on evaluation of its concession. This is dependent on its duration and Hochtief, which is close-mouthed about the matter, is reported to have been demanding an extension.

The 2007 budget said that the government would "develop" its AIA assets without giving details. This has been interpreted by some commentators to mean that the state might offer to extend the concession in exchange for a considerable upfront payment.

Telecoms

The most liberalised network industry in Greece is telecommunications. The Mitsotakis government awarded two foreign investor groups second-generation mobile licences in September 1992 and, after a prolonged rearguard action by successive Pasok administrations to delay EU-mandated market opening, the exclusive right of the state-owned Hellenic Telecommunications Organisation (OTE) to provide fixed-line services was finally terminated as of January 1, 2001.[26]

Today there are some 1,850 firms in the ICT (information and communication technology) sector, 14 percent of them active in various aspects of telecoms.[27]

Even so, according to the regulator, the National Telecommunications and Post Commission (EETT), the market is "still characterised by strong monopolistic features".[28] As of December 31, 2006, OTE continued to command 72 percent market share of fixed telephony and 37 percent of mobile.

There is as yet only a limited amount of alternative backbone to that of OTE and most new carriers piggy-back[29] on its network against the payment of fees.[30]

---

[26] Law 2867/00 amending Law 2246/94. For background, see Robert McDonald, The Competitiveness of the Greek Economy 2005, Athens News [Books], 2005, pp 71-77.

[27] Nikos Kakaris, Study of the ICT Sector in Greece - main results, Observatory for the Greek Information Society, January 30, 2007.

[28] EETT Newsletter, Issue 10, October 2006, p 3.

[29] In 2005 only 1 percent of connections used alternative providers for accessing the public telephone network compared with 7.7 percent in the EU.

[30] In 2006, OTE earned €98.6m from interconnection fees and a further €41.9m from interconnection fees for international calls originating from mobile operators out of its total revenues of €5.9bn.

Table 18. Number of individually licensed providers per activity

Activity	Number of providers
Voice telephony and development of fixed network	103
Voice telephony	102
Development of fixed network	38
Satellite communications	12
2nd-generation mobile telephony[a]	5
3rd-generation mobile telephony[b]	4
TETRA[c]	1
W-LAN[d]	38

[a]*GSM 900 and 1800 in the 10-30MHz bandwidth.* [b]*Mobile broadband in the 5-15MHz bandwidth.* [c]*Terrestrial Trunked Radio Access for special radio communication services through a digital mobile network.* [d]*Public mobile telecommunication services.*

Source: *Annual report 2006*, EETT

The principal reason that the telecoms market is as open as it is arises from the fact that EETT, unlike other Greek regulatory bodies, has been fully staffed and granted operational autonomy. It is unique among the country's regulatory agencies in having been delegated legislative powers.

It operates under the policy guidance of the Ministry of Transport and Communications (YME) but authorises licences in its own right and has powers to issue regulations having statutory force. Operators may appeal its decisions to the administrative courts in the way they might a government decision.

An individual or an entity seeking to enter the telecoms sector makes a declaration of registration to the EETT and a general authorisation is automatic unless the EETT objects within a set time limit and on specific grounds of non-compliance with the terms and the conditions of the law or its own regulations.

EETT charges fees for operating licences, the assignment of radio frequency and other services. These cover its operating costs and still give it funds left over of which it is obliged to consign 80 percent to the state budget, the balance being used for "special actions" determined by YME.

EETT has the right to approve the pricing methodologies utilised by fixed and mobile carriers and to authorise administrative sanctions on providers that breach the law or its regulations and decisions.

OTE has used various tactics to delay opening of its network to alternative providers, principally by charging access fees so high as to make its rivals uncompetitive.

EETT has on several occasions intervened to require the incumbent to reshape aspects of its pricing and in three cases levied fines of between €2m and €3m for failure to open services with sufficient alacrity. In every instance, OTE has exercised its right of appeal and resolution of all the cases is pending.

At the time of writing, OTE was facing damage suits from at least four private operators on grounds that it had defaulted on various market-opening obligations such as the provision of leased lines and carrier preselection for international calls and local and national mobile calls.[31] The cases also are either pending or under appeal in the courts.

The EETT has not applied sanctions to OTE alone. It has also fined mobile companies for failure to comply with the EU's inter-connection directive and for operating a cartel in the pricing of SMS messages.

Directives delayed

In 2002, the European Commission issued six directives (plus additional decisions, recommendations and guidelines) to create the basis of an integrated EU-wide "electronic communications" regulatory framework.[a]

The package encouraged national regulatory authorities to cooperate with the commission in the creation of an EU single market.

Member states were supposed to transpose the directives by July 24, 2003,[b] but both the last Pasok government and the ND administration delayed, leading to the institution of infringement proceedings.

The directives were not transposed until January 2006, becoming law the following month.[c] As of mid-2007, the infringement proceedings remained pending.

The Commission has already moved on to the notion of "functional separation" of networks, ie it is proposing that the former monopolies create separate companies for their network and service activities.[c]

These would be overseen by a super-regulator in Brussels made up of the directors of the 27 EU national telecommunications agencies.

---

[31] *Telepassport (€52.15m). Tellas (€16.5m). Lannet (€1.5m) and Teledome (€14.2m).*

The concept faces considerable industry opposition and the commission may have difficulties securing the necessary political support in the European Council and Parliament to secure approval of directives that would make the concept enforceable.[d]

ᵃDirectives 2002/19/EC on access to, and interconnection of, electronic communications networks and associated facilities; 2002/20/EC on the authorisation of election communications networks and services; 2002/21/EC on a common regulatory network; 2002/22/EC on universal service and users' rights [carriers with Significant Market Power are required to provide services to all customers including those on low income, in rural, insular and high-cost areas at affordable rates]; 2002/58/EC on the processing of personal data and the protection of privacy; and 2002/77/EC on competition in markets. ᵇExcept for the data protection directive for which the deadline was October 31, 2003. ᶜLaw 3431/06. The data protection directive was transposed in June through Law 3471/06. ᶜAs in the electricity and gas industries. ᵈ"EU considers a telecommunications 'super-regulator'", *International Herald Tribune,* August 13, 2007.

Because of Greeks' love affair with their mobile phones, the country in 2005 ranked number 10 out of the 30 member states of the OECD in terms of "total communication access paths". It was number four in the penetration of mobiles with 112 subscribers per 100 inhabitants,[32] compared with an OECD average of 80 but it was sorely deficient in broadband connections.

As recently as January 1, 2004, ADSL connections - 384 kilobytes per second (kbps) to 1,024 kbps (then the highest speed available) - stood at just 0.1 percent of the total number of digital connections because of a lack of ports in the OTE system.

OTE, recognising the profit potential of broadband for the sale of value-added services, has made installation of new ADSL ports a priority and reported that at the end of 2006 it had 759,912 in place with a target by the end of 2007 of 1.2m.[33]

ADSL market penetration at the end of 2006 was put at 512,000 lines, or 4.6 per 100 inhabitants,[34] well below the OECD average of 16.9 and ranking Greece number 28 just marginally ahead of Turkey and Mexico.[35] During the first half of 2007, ADSL connections were

---

[32] *That is to say some subscribers have more than one account. Of the total. 75 per 100 use prepaid cards rather than contract services.*

[33] Annual Report. *Form 20-F. US Securities and Exchange Commission. June 28. 2007. p 26.*

[34] OECD Broadband Statistics 2007, www.oecd.org/sti/ict/broadband.

[35] *Most eurozone partners had penetrations of 20 percent and above.*

reported to have risen by 55 percent to stand at 760,000, a penetration level of 6.9 percent.[36]

This led to (and partly was caused by) inordinately high prices for the service. As recently as 2004, it cost €216.80 a month to get a modest 1,024 kbps connection. By mid-2007 that had fallen to €14.63 a month.

True broadband speeds (2,048bkbps to 8,192 kbps) were available at that time at rates ranging between €17.50 and €37 per month, but such high-speed connections still accounted for only 0.5 pps of the total.[37]

In summer 2007, EETT imposed on OTE a hefty fine of €26.7m (equivalent to 3.1 percent of estimated 2007 earnings after tax) for using its dominant position in the market to thwart new broadband entrants.[38] The company appealed.

The incumbent has been slow in providing local-loop unbundling (LLU), which involves giving alternative operators direct access to the copper co-axial cables in its network. According to EETT data, at the end of June 2007 the LLU penetration in the OTE network was just 1.77 percent, compared with an EU average of 8.44 percent (as on January 1, 2007).[39]

Broadband development programme

In 2006, the Special Secretariat for Digital Planning (an adjunct of the Ministry of Economy and Finance) secured Brussels' approval to launch a Broadband Action Programme.

The scheme, budgeted at €450m, targets penetration of 8 percent by the end of 2008.[a] It forms part of CSF III and is financed 50-50 from EU and national funds.

The programme calls for, among other things, development of metropolitan area broadband networks in 75 cities (€63m); installation of wireless broadband networks in 120 municipalities (€42m); delivery of e-government services by local authorities (€60m); and broadband services and digital TV for the disabled (€50m).

In addition, the state is to co-finance 770 wireless access points in some 400 businesses (€21m) and to invest in the takeup of broadband services on HellasSAT (€10m).

---

[36] *"Broadband Internet use rising fast"*. Kathimerini (English edition). *August 11, 2007.*

[37] Ibid. *The figure is attributed to EETT.*

[38] *"OTE's CEO on recent fine"*. Greek Equities Daily. *Eurobank Securities. August 13, 2007.*

[39] *"Broadband Internet use rising fast"*. Kathimerini (English edition). *August 11, 2007.*

A subprogramme budgeted at €210m is designed to increase geographical coverage to 60 percent and population coverage to 90 percent. It entails spending of €160m to promote infrastructure and access plus €50m on demand stimulation.

The projects in the subprogramme were tendered in September 2006, just three months before the end of CSFIII, and the contracts awarded in February 2007 during the extension period granted to Greece.

Three of the contracts went to Hellas on Line, two to Forthnet and one each to Tellas and CYTA Hellas, the Greek subsidiary of the Cypriot telecoms company.

OTE was excluded from the tender but as part of its drive to expand its ADSL network claims to have sufficient installed points of presence to service all communities of at least 500 people.

[a]Dr Yannis Larios, *Greece - broadband action programme to 2008,* Presentation to Broadband Action Gap 2007, Brussels, May 15, 2007.

The liberalisation of the market has attracted significant investment - the majority of it foreign. The two second-generation (2G) mobile licences sold in August 1992 went for $160m to consortia led by Vodafone of the UK and by Telecom Italia.[40] Their contracts called for them each to invest $600m in rolling out their networks. At the time, it was the largest foreign investment ever made in Greece.

The sale in December 2000 of bandwidth for the creation of LMDS - wireless fixed access[41] - raised just under €60m plus commitments to invest some €500m in rollout, while the sale in July 2001 of bandwidth for UMTS[42] - third-generation (3G) mobiles - produced revenues of €645m plus promises of €3bn in network investments.

Among the companies that acquired LMDS licences were Panafon and Telestet, respectively the local subsidiaries of Vodafone and Telecom Italia (they also bought UMTS licences), while a third went to a consortium of Tellas plus Israeli investors.

Tellas, founded in October 2000, was a joint venture by DEI Telecommunications, a subsidiary of the Public Power Corporation

[40] *For more details see Robert McDonald.* The Competitiveness of the Greek economy 2005. *Athens News [Books] 2005. pp 72-73.*

[41] *Local Multipoint Distributed Services. essentially micro-wave relay.*

[42] *Universal Mobile Telephony System. operating in the 2.1GHz range. allowing the transmission of video and mobile Internet.*

(DEI), that held 50 percent minus one share, and Wind (then a joint venture of Enel, the Italian electricity company, and France Telecom),[43] which held 50 percent plus one share.

Since 2002, Greek telecoms have been caught up in a global game of musical chairs, including buyouts and rapid resales by private equity investors. It is arguable whether this process adds value to the sector but it certainly has attracted significant sums of foreign capital into the Greek economy.

- Vodafone in 2004/05 paid €316m to buy out its Greek partner (Intracom) in Panafon and a further €846m to buy back the company's shares that were listed on the Athens Stock Exchange. Vodafone delisted the Greek company, renamed it and turned it into an operational unit of its global brand.[44]

- Telecom Italia Mobile Group (TIM) in 2002 bought out its US partner in Telestet and renamed the company TIM Hellas.

In April 2005 private equity interests - Apax Partners and Texas Pacific Group paid €1.4bn to acquire TIM Hellas and, that autumn, a further €0.3bn to buy up the fourth 2G mobile licence holder, Q-Telecom.

On February 7, 2007, TIM and Q-Telecom were sold in a quick-flip for €3.4bn[45] to Weather Investments, a vehicle for Naguib Sawiri, head of the Egyptian-based Orascom Group of mobile companies. In 2005, Weather had paid €4.8bn to acquire Wind from Enel (*see Tellas above*). Sawiri renamed TIM Hellas Wind and embarked on a massive advertising campaign designed to improve the company's third-place market share.

- The Public Power Corporation agreed on July 31, 2007 to sell its minority interest in Tellas to Weather (*see TIM above*) for €175m. DEI will retain the fibre optic network already installed,[46] which it will lease to Tellas.

---

[43] *The holdings were Enel 56.6 percent and France Telecom 43.4 percent. In 2003, 100 percent of Wind was acquired by Enel and with it the Tellas stake.*

[44] *Rough estimates suggest that Vodafone's total investment to acquire the licence, to roll out its network and to acquire full control of its subsidiary was in the neighbourhood of €3.5bn, a good part of it FDI, although some of it re-invested profits realised in Greece. Some of the investment made in the share buy-back would have been paid to foreign investors.*

[45] *For €500m in cash and the assumption of €2.9bn in debt.*

[46] *1,600km in the right of way of its transmission lines and 170km in urban areas.*

- Sistema of Russia[47] early in 2006 paid €120m and assumed €440m in debt to acquire 51 percent of Intracom Telecom, the telecommunications arm of the digital equipment manufacturer which used to be one of two main suppliers[48] of switching gear to OTE. According to a press report, Sistema has done a deal to provide a fixed-line platform to Vodafone.[49]

- Intracom Holdings in early 2006 tried to acquire Forthnet, the country's second largest Internet service provider (ISP),[50] but lost a bidding war with Novator Equities, an investment company for Icelandic billionaire Thor Bjorgolfsson.[51]

Subsequently, Intracom Holdings acquired the country's third largest ISP, Hellas on Line (HOL), which had recently acquired a company that had installed a fibre optic ring in the region of Attica. A deal to on-sell 51 percent of HOL for €47.9m to United TeleSystems (Comstar), a subsidiary of Sistema, fell through.[52] (*8)

In August 2007, Intracom acquired Teledome, a provider with a licence to provide fixed-access telephony.[53] Teledome is reported to have 80,000 customers, of which more than half are broadband clients.

In its announcement to the Athens Exchange, Intracom described the move as "a further step towards the strategic goal of Intracom SA Holdings for the creation of a strong business group in the sector of integrated telecommunications services".[54] (*8)

The shuffling in the telecoms sector will continue for some time although the focus in the short term will be on smaller players. HOL, Forthnet and Tellas will get a fillip to their business from participation in the government's Broadband Action Programme (*see inset on page 136*).

---

[47] A private sector conglomerate of service-based companies, the largest in the CIS, founded in 1993, it has interests in, among other things, telecoms, banking, tourism, real estate and media. www.sistema.com.[48] The other being the Greek subsidiary of Siemens of Germany.

[49] "Marfin set to buy Greek telco", Athens News, July 27, 2007.

[50] The largest is OTEnet, 94.6 percent owned by OTE with the balance of the shares held by various academic institutions.

[51] It acquired a 34.3 percent blocking minority interest in Forthnet.

[52] The deal signed in December 2006 was subject to approval by the Greek regulatory authorities by June 30, 2007. When these were not forthcoming, the transaction was "discontinued". www.comstar-uts.ru. Comstar made its announcement on July 6, 2007. On July 9, 2007, EETT announced that it had issued a decision clearing the deal.

[53] "Intracom to add Teledome to its telecom armory", Kathimerini (English edition), July 27, 2007.

[54] Intracom SA Holdings, Announcement, Athens Exchange, August 13, 2007.

The next large-scale deal will come if the newly elected government is prepared fully to privatise OTE/Cosmote. Orange, the global mobile subsidiary of France Telecom, is known to have had its eye on the Greek market for some time. (*9)

Energy

Refining and petroleum products

The Greek oil products sector typifies the Greek phenomenon of a market that is at one and the same 'free' and yet restricted.

Refining is a duopoly between state-controlled Hellenic Petroleum (ELPE) and the privately-owned[55] Motor Oil Hellas, though control of ELPE may pass to the private sector as early as 2008 (*see page 142*).

There are some 20 wholesale trading companies, but the market is dominated by EKO, a subsidiary of ELPE, and the multinationals BP and Shell.

The retail market is open. A limited number of stations are owned by trading companies. The majority are run by owner-operators who acquire their brand affiliations through supply agreements with traders who set certain business standards in exchange for the use of their name. The market is significantly overpumped with 8,300 petrol stations for some 6m road vehicles (cars, trucks and motorcycles).

The legislation governing the market keeps wholesale prices artificially high, but the state until recently has applied the lowest level of excise duties within the EU which has helped to keep retail prices low. The tax rate is being increased as part of an EU harmonisation scheme, something to which the ND government has not been entirely averse given its need to find new revenue sources, though it is concerned about the impact on inflation.

Ruthless competition at the retail level keeps forecourt prices low but also drives unscrupulous operators to cut corners and to sell heating and agricultural diesel as road fuel and petrol diluted with all sorts of chemicals (even with water) in order to secure profits from slim margins. It is also alleged that there is considerable collusion among retailers, particularly in the provinces, to keep prices high.

The state still has extraordinary powers to intervene in markets to prevent price distortions (particularly in the mountains and on the

---

[55] *Vardinoyannis family interests include, among other things, refining, petroleum products retailing, shipping (tankers), media (Star television) and banking (Piraeus Bank).*

islands, and particularly during the tourist season or times of exceptional weather conditions), though these have been used sparingly.

Under the leadership of Andreas Papandreou, socialist governments pursued the French and Italian model of creating state enterprises that were 'national champions'. The Public Petroleum Corporation (DEP) was one of the socialists' pet projects modelled on Agip in Italy and Elf in France.

In 1984, the refining and retailing assets of Esso-Pappas in Thessaloniki were added to those of the Aspropyrgos Refinery (ELDA) to create an integrated production and sales organisation. In 1988 the Public Gas Corporation (DEPA) was created as a wholly-owned subsidiary to manage the development of natural gas imports and to create a national grid and distribution network.

The socialists fought a long battle with Brussels to forestall liberalising the petroleum market and paid heavy fines under infringement proceedings rather than implement policies that might have compromised domination of the market by the state-owned refineries. In 1992, the ND government freed retail prices.

In 1998, the sprawling holdings of DEP were reorganised and streamlined as a corporation, Hellenic Petroleum, and the company was part-privatised by listing on the Athens and London stock exchanges.[56] Since, successive governments gradually have listed further tranches until the state stake today has been reduced to a blocking minority of 35.48 percent.[57]

In 2003, the Latsis Group[58] acquired a 24.7 percent stake in ELPE through the merger of its Petrola refinery at Elefsis with the state-controlled company. It has since taken its shareholding to 35.89 percent through its Luxembourg-based company Paneuropean Oil and Industrial Holdings. The merger agreement allows that after October 1, 2008, the board may be elected freely by 50 percent plus one share of the registered shareholders. The implicit, albeit unwritten, commitment is that management will pass to the Latsis group. Since the undertaking

---

[56] The bulk of the shareholding in DEPA, which carried heavy debt associated with its investment in the natural gas network, was returned to the state so as not to be a burden on the share price.

[57] For background see Robert McDonald, "Lacklustre energy", Special Survey 61, Business File, Kerkyra Publications, Athens, October 2006 and Robert McDonald, "A new energy era", Special Survey No 43, Business File, March 2002.

[58] Their interests include, among other things, banking (EFG Eurobank), property (Lamda Development and Eurobank Properties), shipping and refining.

was given by a Pasok government and ND is presumed to embrace private sector ownership, the assumption is that this commitment will not be reversed.

Following the merger, ELPE owns three of the country's four refineries and commands 73 percent of refining capacity. It also controls some 6.56m cubic metres of the country's 8.76m cubic metres of crude and products storage capacity.[59]

The fourth refinery is owned by Motor Oil (Hellas), which sells about half its production on the inland market and trades about half overseas. Between them, the two companies supply 86 percent of the Greek wholesale market.[60]

Under legislation passed in 1995[61] to comply with EU rules, oil companies are required to maintain security stocks equivalent to 90 days of their sales in the previous year. Most trading companies did not have sufficient tankage to meet this obligation and so sought to store with the refining companies. The refineries would only do this, however, if a trading company were a customer, effectively making it captive.

In 2001, the European Court of Justice ruled this practice to be incompatible with EU competition law, and the following year the Pasok government introduced legislation[62] which reduced the stocks of trading companies to just five days and said that these could be held under contracts with refineries not related to supply.[63] Product importers were still required to hold the 90-day strategic stocks.[64]

Trading companies have considered constructing their own tank farms to hold such stocks but found the capital and operating costs too expensive. They thus store the bulk of their imports, including their mandatory reserves, with the refineries at a cost of the order of $23 a tonne.

---

[59] *The principal assets of the Petrola refinery at the time of the merger were its tank farm, the largest in southeast Europe with storage capacity of 3.34m cubic metres, and its truck-loading facility with annual throughput capacity of 1.2m tonnes. The refinery itself was a basic topping unit producing kerosene and gasoil. It is currently the subject of a major upgrade programme.*

[60] *Marina Spyridaki. Aspects of an evolving national regulatory regime: the case of the market for petroleum products in Greece, 3rd Hellenic Observatory PhD Symposium, June 14-15, 2007.*

[61] *Law 2289/95.*

[62] *Law 3054/02.*

[63] *The legislation also allowed large retailers to form consortia to buy directly from refineries, though they too had to have storage facilities for security stocks. Previously only the armed forces, Olympic Airways and the Public Power Corporation had been able to buy direct from the refineries.*

[64] *For the refineries this included both crude and products imported for resale.*

In 2005, ND amended the oil law.[65] Companies may obtain finished products from any source, domestic or foreign,[66] on the sole condition that they pay taxes in accord with EU directives on imports from third countries. The requirement remains, however, that they must maintain strategic stocks equal to 90/365ths of the previous year's sales by product.

Multinational trading companies claim that they could import products from their refineries in neighbouring countries (Italy in particular) at prices cheaper than they have to pay in Greece but say that the cost of storage makes it cheaper to buy domestically refined products.

The result is that the refineries and trading companies import only specialty products (such as lubes) or products that are in short supply (such as gasoil).

Electricity & Gas

In the post-WWII era in Europe, the provision of electricity and gas was principally the province of vertically integrated, state-owned monopolies that provided, distributed and sold their products to captive customers.

For the past decade, the European Commission, as part of its efforts to create the single internal market, has been pursuing market opening and competition both within member states and across borders with a view to allowing consumers freedom of choice in supply.

To this end, the commission has sought to separate production and imports from delivery networks and to create wholesale and retail markets. A brace of directives in 1996 (electricity) and 1998 (gas), elaborated and extended by a further pair in 2003[67], required:

- creation of separate companies to operate the former monopoly-owned electricity grids and natural gas pipeline networks - transmission and distribution system operators (TSOs and DSOs);

- third-party access (TPA) to these systems with market-oriented tariffs but under the close supervision of regulators to ensure equal access;

- establishment of wholesale markets in which both state-owned companies and private operators compete;

- unbundling of the accounts of the former integrated monopoly

---

[65] *Law 3335/05.*

[66] *Greece imports some products from Russian refineries.*

[67] Directive 03/54/EC *on electricity and* 03/55/EC *on gas.*

providers so that transactions between their various divisions reflect true costs in order to prevent cross-subsidies that might allow them to offer predatory, market-distorting prices; and

- opening of retail markets so that customers could choose their supplier - by July 1, 2004 for large consumers and by July 1, 2007 for all customers including households.

The process was supposed to begin in 1999 and most member states complied in one way or another. Italy, eg, launched the state-owned power company Enel on the stock market and forced it to sell a third of its generating capacity. This was bought by Edison, a consortium of Italian interests together with Électricité de France.

The policy achieved liberalisation and privatisation more or less in one go, left the state holding a third of Enel and created two major players in the Italian market. Enel gained large cash resources, which it subsequently invested in energy companies in a dozen other countries. Edison, after consolidation in the domestic market, has become a player abroad and is poised to become a major investor in Greece (*see pages 156-157*).

Other EU member states used different techniques such as having the incumbent outsource plants to private market participants (Ireland) or having private firms build plants to the incumbent's specifications and then renting them the assets (Portugal).

In larger member states such as the UK, France, Germany and Spain there was a spate of cross-border mergers and acquisitions between large, integrated electricity and gas companies so that French interests now have presence in the UK, Belgian and Spanish in France and German in Spain.

The Pasok government, which was in power in Greece at the time the Commission commenced the process, resisted liberalisation. It secured derogations for the opening of the electricity market until February 19, 2001 and for natural gas until November 15, 2006.

In the electricity sector it claimed that it needed time to modernise the Public Power Corporation (DEI) to prepare it for privatisation, a process which finally commenced in December 2001.

In the sector of natural gas, it pleaded that, as Greece was an emerging market (it took its first deliveries in 1996), the Public Gas Corporation (DEPA) needed time to properly establish a customer base that would allow it to amortise the €1.5bn investment it made to construct the high- and medium-pressure network.

It went through the motions of legal compliance, but in practice dragged out implementation in such a way as to prolong monopoly control and thwart market opening.

In 1999, the government passed legislation[68] which introduced a liberalised market on paper. It provided for

- licensed Independent Power Producers (IPPs) to compete with DEI (which would lose its monopoly and in theory become just another licensed operator);

- management of the transmission grid by a company to be known as the Hellenic Transmission System Operator (DESMIE); and

- a Regulatory Authority for Energy (RAE) to advise the government on policy and licensing and to oversee market operations.

It was not, however, until the end of 2000, under mounting pressure from the commission, that the government finally tendered private power generation licences.

There was an overwhelming response: 921 bids totalling 19,600MW of installed capacity, nearly one and a half times the production capacity then installed on the grid.

In the course of 2001, eleven IPPs were issued thermal-generating licences with installed capacity of 3,100MW - equal to about 28 percent of the total capacity in the system. The DESMIE, established in March 2001, began to function that May.

Theoretically, the IPPs could have constructed their generating plants and a market could have begun to function by around 2003, only four years behind the EU schedule. The problem was that the wholesale mechanism was fashioned in such a way that private operators could not secure a return on their investment in under 20 years. Most banks will not lend beyond ten - 12 at the outside. Thus the IPPs were forced to postpone their projects while they lobbied for the law's recasting.

The then Minister of Development, with responsibility for energy, was Akis Tsohadzopoulos, a decided opponent of liberalisation. He dragged his feet for nearly two years and it was not until June 2003 - the same month that the EU introduced its new set of directives requiring even further market opening - that he brought forward legislation[69] to implement the 1999 provisions.

---

[68] *Law 2773/99.*
[69] *Law 3175/03.*

To create space in the market for the IPPs, this law prohibited DEI from expanding its capacity till the end of the decade, although it was to be permitted to replace 1,600MWof its old, polluting lignite-burning plant, with new gas-fired or clean, hard coal-burning units.[70] Additionally, it was to unbundle its accounts between its mining, generation, transmission and sales divisions in order to promote price transparency.

The wholesale market - a despatch and contract-clearing pool managed by DESMIE - was restructured in such a way that independent producers were supposed to be able to secure prices to allow them to pay down their debt within 12 years.

If they could not, and to ensure sufficient private capacity soon enough to guarantee system stability, DESMIE was to be allowed to offer subsidised payments designed to cover capital risk for up to 900MW of private plant.[71]

The IPPs were supposed to be able freely to choose their gas supplier from July 1, 2005, which implied that the gas market would also be opened and that DEPA's monopoly on imports would be ended nearly a year and a half earlier than foreseen under the gas derogation.

The problem was that while prices would rise in the wholesale market, they were not to be freed in the retail. Government has the right administratively to set tariffs so long as DEI has a 70 percent market share - the rationale being that this allows it to intervene to prevent the incumbent abusing its dominant position to apply in ordinate price hikes.

Successive governments have retained the right because they believe that it is to their political advantage to keep prices low. The average price of power in Greece is about half that in the rest of the EU25.

The EU electricity directive was predicated on the notion that there would be several retail supply companies buying power from the wholesale market and that competition would eventually bring down prices.

In Greece, however, DEI as yet is the sole retail provider. Thus, not only was it going to have to stand aside to make room for the new

---

[70] *The redundant plants would be placed in cold reserve under the control of DESMIE in order to guarantee security of supply in the system.*

[71] *Provided that these units were fuelled with natural gas and located in the south of the country where there was a capacity deficiency.*

generators, but under the market mechanism devised it was also going to have to pay them higher prices to support their entry into the wholesale market while being forced to cap its retail rates because of government price determination.

Understandably, the incumbent lobbied intensively against the new measures and, because government was not anxious to promote liberalisation in the first place, implementation dragged. The head of the Regulatory Authority resigned because of the lack of progress.[72]

In the natural gas sector, the socialists allowed DEPA to retain its monopoly over the high- and medium-pressure transmission networks (through which gas is imported overland from Russia) and the liquefied natural gas terminal on the island of Revythoussa, some 50km offshore Athens (through which LNG is imported by sea from Algeria).

As well as its monopoly on supply to electricity generators until mid-2005, DEPA retained the exclusive right to supply all industrial users consuming volumes in excess of 10 million cubic metres a year.

The retail gas market was 'liberalised' in 1999/2000 by the creation of three companies to service commercial and household customers that consumed less than 10m cubic metres a year. (There was virtually no such market then and, even today, the split of DEPA's sales is approximately 70 percent power producers, 20 percent industrial users and 10 percent the retail companies.)

DEPA created a wholly-owned subsidiary, the Gas Distribution Company (EDA), to own the limited low-pressure distribution network. Tenders were called seeking experienced international operators to participate in three joint ventures - Gas Supply Companies (EPA) - that would be owned 51 percent by EDA and 49 percent by the private interests.

The private groups paid a lump sum upfront[73] to acquire the marketing concessions and committed to work programmes to roll out further distribution networks, which they would finance. Once completed, the network infrastructure became the property of EDA. DEPA's contribution to the JVs was the distribution licence.

A consortium comprised of 60 percent Cinergy Global Power Inc

---

[72] See Robert McDonald. The Competitiveness of the Greek Economy 2005. Athens News [Books]. 2005. p 87.

[73] Attica €160.9m: Thessaloniki €150.8m: and Thessaly €39.9m.

(the UK subsidiary of Cinergy of Cincinnati[74]) and 40 percent Shell Gas BV of the Netherlands secured the concession for Attica, while Italgas took the two for Thessaloniki and Thessaly.

The concessions gave the EPAs exclusive right to use the network for 30 years to 2030. DEPA was to be their exclusive wholesale supplier.

During the period 2001-03, the Simitis government, using its typical privatisation salami tactics, sold three tranches of Public Power Corporation stock on the Athens and London stock exchanges, raising close to €1.5bn.[75] This reduced the state stake to 55 percent - 51.12 percent held directly and the balance controlled indirectly through the company's pension fund, the Public Power Corporation Personnel Insurance Organisation.[76]

In September 2002, the government launched a tender to sell a strategic stake of 35 percent in the Public Gas Corporation. There were nine expressions of interest but, when the tender concluded in September 2003, there was only one firm bidder, Gas Natural of Spain, which reportedly offered some €285m for the stake plus the management.

The socialist government signed a memorandum of understanding with Gas Natural shortly before the March 2004 elections but final negotiations were not complete when Pasok lost the poll.

Thus, by the time of the change of government, there had been no physical liberalisation of Greek energy markets. The state retained strategic control of DEI and DEPA and both companies retained effective monopolies.

In opposition, the ND party had claimed that one of its priorities would be to create a free market in energy. In government it has behaved much as its socialist predecessor, aligning the Greek legislative regime with the EU directives - so compliance can be claimed - but moving at a snail's pace to introduce market opening.

It took the Ministry of Development some 20 months to produce in December 2005 two pieces of legislation[77] that finally transposed the 2003 directives.

---

[74] *Subsequently merged with Duke Energy of Houston, Texas.*

[75] *December 2001, 15.6 percent (€463.7m); December 2002, 13.2 percent (€357m); and October 2003, 15.7 percent (€636m).*

[76] *For background see Robert McDonald, The Competitiveness of the Greek Economy 2005, Athens News [Books], 2005, pp 81-94 and Robert McDonald, "Lacklustre energy", Special Survey No 61, Business File, October 2006, pp 37-43.*

[77] *Law 3426/05 (electricity) and Law 3428/05 (gas).*

These retained the July 1, 2007 date for the opening of the retail electricity market, but included further derogations for gas that put off opening for light industrial and commercial customers until November 15, 2008 and for household customers until November 15, 2009.

The 2003 directives required that operation of low-pressure distribution (as well as high- and medium-pressure transmission) networks be transferred from incumbents to private operators. The assets *per se* were considered a natural monopoly and could be retained.

In the electricity sector, the Greek legislation provided that DESMIE, the transmission system operator, should take over as DSO as of July 1, 2007.[78] Some 150 staff were seconded from DEI to create an operating unit. (By the handover date they were to choose which company they wanted to work for.) As compensation, DEI became the permanent 49 percent shareholder in DESMIE.[79] DEI continues to own the grid assets, which it leases to DESMIE, and which it must maintain and expand according to DESMIE's instructions.

The wholesale market began to function in summer 2005, though its only participants were DEI, importers and a small peak-shaving unit[80] then operating on contract to DESMIE.

There were no retailers using the market other than DEI. The idea was to gain familiarity with tendering and despatching procedures in order to permit market determination of the wholesale price (the so-called system marginal price) once the IPPs became operational.

The pricing methodology had to be revamped as soon as the first of these entered the market. This was T-Power, owned by Hellenic Petroleum,[81] which commenced operations on Christmas Eve 2005. DEI, using the cheap lignite-burning capacity in its generating mix, proved able to manipulate the mechanism in such a way that the gas-fired operator could not secure a price for its power that allowed it to operate at a profit.

---

[78] *DESMEI rents the electricity network from DEI but has powers to direct DEI on how it must be developed and expanded. This always assumes that DEI can find the funding to carry out the works.*

[79] *When the operating company was originally created, the shareholding was 51 percent state and 49 percent DEI with the proviso that new market entrants would assume a portion of that shareholding (in proportion to their market share) once they had achieved a market share of 5 percent.*

[80] *Heron Thermoelectric, a 147MW quick-starting open-cycle plant constructed as backup for the power system at the time of the Olympic Games.*

[81] *The 390MW combined-cycle, gas-fired generating plant is based at Sindos in Thessaloniki.*

The ND legislation maintained the existing moratorium on the expansion of DEI's generating capacity, but increased the amount of IPP installed capacity[82] that could be subsidised from 900MW to 1,200MW. There were to be three tenders, each for 400MW of capacity, in which DESMIE would be allowed to guarantee a price for the output of up to 280MW with a view to covering their risk on capital cost. The private interests assumed the market and other risks for the remaining 120MW.

After intense wrangling over terms of reference, a schedule was finally set that called for tenders in May and December 2006 and April 2007. It was claimed that Brussels had cleared the process.

The IPPs complained that they were being asked to bid in the absence of some of the secondary legislation regarding the electricity and gas markets so that they could not properly fine-tune their offers. The deadline for submissions in the first tender was postponed from November 2006 to the third week of February 2007.

In April 2007 it was reported that the best bid was made by Enelco, a 75-25 joint venture between Enel of Italy and the Kopelouzos Group, which has gas import rights through Prometheus Gas, a partnership with Russia's Gazprom. An underbidder raised objections[83] and the adjudication was frozen pending review by European Commission authorities.[84]

Gas liberalisation was also plagued with complications. Although the Pasok legislation of 2003 had allowed that power producers should be able to choose an alternative supplier to DEPA by July 2005, this proved impossible because third-party access tariffs (TPA) were not introduced until March 2006,[85] nine months after the deadline. Even these are provisional until 2009, which made it difficult for the IPPs to make longterm cost projections in their tenders.

The TPA tariff is structured in such a way that the burden of the charge (90 percent) applies to users of the overland high-pressure

[82] *Extending the moratorium until 2011.*

[83] *Both Enelco and GEK-Terna were said to have requested subsidy of €35.000 per MW but Enelco proposed to construct 430MW and GEK-Terna 399MW. Corinth Power, a 70-30 owned consortium of Iberdrola of Spain and Motor Oil Hellas, is reported to have raised objections. "Candidate in the HTSO tender for the new natgas plant reportedly raised objections".* Greek Equities Daily, EFG Eurobank Securities, April 13, 2007.

[84] *"Power deregulation only on paper".* Kathimerini (English edition), July 11, 2007.

[85] *Ministerial decision 4955, March 27, 2006.*

network. Thus any competitor to DEPA will, in the short term at least, be forced by economics to import LNG. For the time being, this is not possible because of the limitations of the terminal's storage capacity.

To comply with the directive's requirement that there be separation of network management, ND's 2005 gas law called for the creation, by December 2006,[86] of a new company, the Hellenic Gas Transmission System Operator (DESFA), that would own and operate the transmission system. DESFA is wholly owned by DEPA, though the government is to vote its shares and appoint its executives for the first decade of operations in order to ensure 'autonomy'.

The low-pressure distribution system remained under the ownership of DEPA's wholly-owned subsidiary EDA.

The 2005 legislation provided for EDA to become the majority shareholder in three new EPAs that are to construct distribution networks and provide retail gas services in central and eastern Macedonia and in Sterea Hellada/Evia.[87] To prevent the creation of new monopolies, the Commission insisted that these should have the right to choose their gas supplier from inception - always assuming that there is one other than DEPA at the time they commence operations.

As of November 2008, the three existing EPAs, if they have needs that exceed their present contracts with DEPA, will also be free to choose their supplier, though this seems unlikely as till now they have consistently fallen short of their existing offtake quotas.

Also from November 2008, non-household customers (ie light industries and commercial premises) without an agreement with an existing EPA will be free to chose their supplier, assuming there is an alternative.

From November 2009, domestic customers' suppliers residing outside the territories of the EPAs, will be free to choose a supplier, although the number of these will be few. Regions falling outside the geographical reach of the EPAs are sparsely populated, making the establishment of local retail companies to service them unlikely.[88]

---

[86] *It is not clear when it was incorporated but its board of directors was not nominated until April 2007.*

[87] *DEPA has been granted a fourth distribution and supply licence for the Prefecture of Corinth, according to the law firm KGDI (Kyriakides Georgopoulos & Daniolos Issaias) which prepared the Greek submission to Gas Regulation 2007, a comparative international legal guide, by Global Legal Group of the UK, www.ICLG.co.uk.*

[88] *Except perhaps on the islands of Crete and Rhodes which will be open to competition and could be serviced by private LNG terminals - though the payback period would be extended given the costs involved.*

The ND government allowed Pasok's near-complete privatisation deal with Gas Natural to lapse. Under its own privatisation schedule it announced that DEPA would be floated on the Athens Stock Exchange during 2007.[89] At the time of writing, this had not happened and the idea appeared to have been abandoned for the time being.

Thus, eight years after energy liberalisation was legally supposed to have commenced:

- the state maintains majority control of DEI and remains the sole owner of DEPA;

- a 'liberalised' market has been legislated, but DEI commands 92 percent of electricity sales[90] and DEPA 100 percent of natural gas;

- the proposed mechanism to subsidise the entry of IPPs into the market is in limbo pending European Commission rulings;

- there are no private sector retailers of electricity; DEI is still the sole source for households; and

- while private gas companies could in theory enter the market to supply IPPs and even DEI (it holds an option to acquire 30 percent of DEPA which it seeks to exercise), the TPA regime is such that economically they would have to import LNG, and this cannot happen before 2008 at the earliest because of storage constraints at the terminal.

The Regulatory Authority for Energy has described Revythoussa as "the most suitable entry point for new players in the Greek gas market... [and] is expected to be the cornerstone for the development of competition".[91]

The facility is being expanded and by 2008 its send-out capacity should treble. Furthermore, there is consideration being given to nearly doubling its current underground storage capacity ($130,000m^3$) through the addition of a $120,000m^3$ of surface tankage.

Meanwhile, the electricity supply system is stretched to capacity and urgently in need of expansion.

At the end of 2006 there were 13,230MW of installed capacity in the system - including the units of DEI (12,695MW) and two private producers T-Power (390MW) and Heron Thermoelectric (147MW).

International practice is that there should be 15 percent spare capacity in the system to allow for downtime for maintenance and

---

[89] Press reports spoke of a modest 15 percent.

[90] This is DEI's estimate; the European Commission has put it as high as 96 percent.

[91] Legal Framework of the Greek Natural Gas Market, www.rae.gr.

possible plant failures, ie the Greek system should expect only 11,250MW of plant to be available at any one time.

Each summer since 2005, demands on the system have reached new record levels, the peak so far being 10,610 MW on July 23, 2007. This leaves the network dangerously close to capacity and increasingly unstable. In 2005, there was a mismatch that led to a massive outage that blacked out much of the south of the country.

The Ministry of Development says that the problems are being addressed through improved network management but at least some of its measures smack of make-do rather than policy designed to create a system capable of satisfying demand.

For example, each summer since 2005, YPAN has offered high-voltage industrial users subsidies to reduce their consumption. This means concomitant cuts in their production.

In summer 2007 public servants were sent home early on a number of occasions to save electricity, while there were programmed cuts of power to entire small towns and to districts of larger cities to prevent another debilitating system collapse.

Demand projections suggest that at least one new 400MW plant should be coming on stream each year between now and the end of the decade and perhaps beyond.

Given the delay in the subsidised IPP tenders, it will be fourth quarter 2009 at the earliest - more likely considerably later - that the first private power plant might be up and running.

In June 2007, the Ministry of Development tabled an amendment to its legislation saying that DEI should be allowed to replace another 800MW of capacity by 2017, bringing its new and more efficient plant to 2,400MW.[92] (*10)

At the beginning of July, RAE went through the motions of declaring the electricity market to be fully open. It said that all consumers - including households - were free to choose their supplier,[93] except that there were no alternatives to DEI.

---

[92] DEI will have to decommission 800MW of existing plant unlike the 1,600MW that is to be put in cold reserve with access by DESMIE.

[93] Governments have imposed on DEI the responsibility of collecting through its billing system various charges such as municipal taxes, the licence fee for state TV and a surcharge designed to raise funds for the development of RES. The announcement said that DEI would for at least a year continue to provide billing services (against fees) for alternative suppliers so that such collections would not be disrupted.

In August the government announced its last tariff increase before the general election, an average of 3.3 percent for the year, just above projected annual inflation, and well down from the figure of a year earlier of 4.8 percent, which at the time had been the meagre response to a DEI request for an 8 percent increase to help meet rising fuel costs at a time of soaring world oil prices.

All this said, DEI finally has begun a process of market orientation. Under a new chief executive[94] who took over in March 2007, its charter was amended to separate those areas of its business that are subject to competition and those that are not. The company planned to create one management committee for networks and another for mining, generation and trading, with separate deputy CEOs for each.[95]

In the second quarter of 2007, unbundled accounts were published for the business year 2006. These revealed the true magnitude of the losses sustained by having to provide, under government direction, power at uniform prices across the country - particularly in the non-interconnected islands.

The EU electricity directives say that if governments wish to control prices for social reasons, they should do this under public service orders (PSOs) and that the generating companies should be reimbursed from budgetary funds.

DEI's losses from its public service obligations in 2006 alone amounted to €294m. The power company claimed that it should be reimbursed retroactively to the beginning of the decade when the directive was first supposed to be applied. This would mean a rebate of the order of €1.5bn - perhaps more.

Under ND's 2005 electricity law, the government was supposed to publish a schedule of public service obligations within six months; nearly two years on it has yet to do so.

There is no guarantee that it will reimburse DEI now that the true state of the company's losses has been determined and retroactive compensation seems highly unlikely given the problems the government already has in balancing its budget. But perhaps a start has been made towards rationalising domestic pricing. (*11)

---

[94] The third since ND took office.
[95] "PPC published set of charter amendments, to be proposed to AGM", Greek Equities Daily, EFG Eurobank Securities, June 7, 2007.

The European Commission, in a working document published at the beginning of 2007,[96] concluded that "the prospects of developing a competitive market in Greece are [small]...The regulated price market and the tendering procedure do not deliver sustainability, security of supply and competitiveness in the market. In addition to that the market model...creates obstacles to new entrants...

"The only way forward to bring competition into the Greek market is the integration of this market into the regional one comprised of the South East Europe neighbouring countries. The Energy Community Treaty [*see inset below*] provides for the vehicle to make this happen."

The South East Europe Energy Regulatory Process

As part of the European Commission's evolution of relations with the Balkans, the region is gradually being incorporated into the Internal Energy Market.

In November 2002, a memorandum of understanding was signed in Athens creating the South East Europe Energy Regulation Forum. In October 2005, this was upgraded by the signing of a full treaty, the Energy Community Treaty, by which the acquis communautaire *regarding energy is to be implemented throughout the region.*

The signatories included Albania, Bosnia and Herzegovina, Bulgaria, Croatia, the Former Yugoslav Republic of Macedonia, Montenegro, Romania and Serbia. UNMIK signed on behalf of Kosovo. Turkey has observer status.

The EU energy market directives of 2003 are to be implemented in the participating countries. Non-household customers are to be free to choose their supplier by January 1, 2008 and all customers by January 1, 2015. The treaty establishes obligations regarding pollution controls to be introduced during the period 2011-2017.

Once completed, the project is supposed to create an integrated regional market of some 55m customers. Studies have suggested that up to 2020, 13,500MW of new generating capacity will be needed to meet demand and that 11,500MW of existing plant will have to be upgraded to meet EU environmental standards.

---

[96] Commission staff working document [to accompany] … Prospects for the internal gas and electricity market. *SEC 2006/1709/final. Brussels, January 11, 2007.*

To this end companies holding private generating licences have begun to form alliances with major European players with a view to securing sufficient resources to allow them to become exporters to the Balkans. Recently formed partnerships include:

- A €1.2bn joint venture, Endesa Hellas, between Mytilineos, the mining and mineral processing company (49.99 percent), and Endesa of Spain (50.01 percent). Mytilineos is to contribute its existing energy assets and licences and Endesa €600m in cash.[97] The company will have a mixed portfolio including:

  - a 334MW co-generation plant that Mytilineos has constructed to provide power for its aluminium smelter at Agios Nikolaos, Viotia;

  - a 430MW gas-fired plant under construction at the same site, scheduled for completion in June 2009; and

  - a proposed 600MW fluidised-bed coal plant, also at the Agios Nikolaos energy centre.

  Mytilineos has a 310MW electricity energy trading licence, a pipeline of RES projects totalling 1,000MW, plus two more thermal, generating licences - one for gas and one for imported coal.

- A 50-50 joint venture between Edison of Italy and Hellenic Petroleum. ELPE will contribute T-Power, its 390MW combined-cycle, gas-fired plant at Thessaloniki,[98] and Edison €55m, plus its 65 percent participation in a 420MW gas-fired plant under development by Thisvi Power[99] in Viotia and its licence for a 600MW coal-fired plant at Astakos, the private port on the west coast of the mainland.

  Edison and DEPA are 80-20 partners in a joint venture which is developing a €1.2bn to €1.8bn, 8bn-10bn m³ natural gas pipeline that is designed to carry Caspian, Iranian and Iraqi gas to Europe via Turkey, Greece and Italy. The scheme calls for

  - a 300km inter-connector between the Turkish and Greek systems;

  - a 590km link from Rodopi to Igoumenitsa; and

---

[97] *In October 2006, Metka, the mechanical and civil engineering subsidiary of Mytilineos, signed a strategic cooperation agreement with Alstom, the French electrical equipment manufacturer. It is bidding for contract work as part of the DEI upgrade programme. In July 2007, Metka won a €219m contract to construct a 427MW gas-fired plant for DEI at Aliveri on the large island of Evia that lies just off the east coast of the mainland.*

[98] *Which carried a debt burden of €223m as of December 2006.*

[99] *The other partners in Thisvi are Hellenic Energy & Development (a subsidiary of a joint venture formed by the construction company Elleniki Technodomiki and the telecoms manufacturer Intracom) and the metallurgy company Viohalco, which owns the site.*

- a 212km undersea pipeline to Italy, to be known as the Poseidon Pipeline.

The terrestrial section is scheduled for completion in 2012, the submarine in 2014.

- The acquisition by Iberdrola of Spain of Greek wind-farm developer Rokas and the announcement of plans to invest €2.4bn in 1,640MW of wind farms on eastern Aegean islands (Hios, Lemnos, Lesvos). Plans call for the company to construct two large submarine cables to off-take the power, one to Thrace and the other to Evia and thence to Lavrio. In addition, Iberdrola paid an undisclosed sum in July 2006 to take a 70 percent stake in Corinth Power, the Vardinoyannis-owned IPP, which holds a licence for a 396MW gas-fired power station and which was one of the bidders in the DESMIE tender.

- A 50-50 partnership, Prometheus Gas, formed between the energy-specialist contractors Kopelouzos and Gazexport, the overseas sales arm of Gazprom. Prometheus has import rights from Gazprom as far as the Greek border and could become the first alternative gas supplier in Greece, although the way in which the TPA regime favours entry via the LNG terminal mitigates against overland imports.

Damco Energy, a company owned by Kopelouzos interests, partners Enel of Italy (25-75) in Enelco, a company that holds at least two licences for gas-fired generating plant, one in Viotia and another in Thrace. Enelco was the preferred bidder in the first IPP subsidy tender *(see page 150).*

- A possible alliance between construction and energy group GEK/Terna and Austrian interests. GEK/Terna owns Heron Thermoelectric, which constructed the 147MW plant at Thiva to provide system backup for the grid during the Olympic Games. Heron also is developing a 420MW gas-fuelled plant and working on licensing a 460MW coal-fired plant. Terna's RES division has 109MW of wind farms in operation, 73MW of wind and micro-hydro under construction and nearly 1,600MW of wind and 180MW of hydro under development or in the pipeline.

In December 2006, Verbund, Austria's largest utility (which holds a Greek import-export licence in a joint venture with the Greek firm Energa) announced that it was planning to establish an independent presence in Greece, though it gave no details. According to a *Reuters* report,[100] it was planning to invest €400m to acquire GEK's portfolio,

---

[100] *"Verbund to launch power production in Greece".* Kathimerini (English edition). *December 15, 2006.*

but nothing since has been heard of the deal. It may have fallen through as GEK has since leased the Thiva plant to DEI.

Kyoto & RES

The United Nations Framework Convention on Climate Change (the so-called Kyoto Protocol), which took effect on February 16, 2005,[a] set a longterm objective of stabilising greenhouse gases to prevent global warming.

Under its terms, industrialised countries committed to cut by 2012 their CO_2 emissions by 5.2 percent on average relative to their 1990 levels. The EU accepted a collective target of 8 percent under a burden-sharing arrangement wherein some member states adopted substantial reductions while others, because of their low level of industrial development, were allowed to increase them but below an assigned ceiling.

Greece was allowed to increase its levels by 25 percent - less if possible. In 2004, the last year for which figures are available, Greece had already increased its levels by 24 percent. By the time the protocol took effect, the country had probably already exceeded its target and environmental campaigners have suggested that, unless radical measures are taken, the level could exceed 40 percent by 2012.

To promote compliance, EU member states were assigned global emission levels under a so-called National Allocation Plan. Governments were to conduct an inventory of the emissions from heavily polluting industries such as power plants, refineries, chemical works and steel mills and assign them emissions credits. If they exceeded these, they were to pay a fine of €40/tonne of excess as a goad to make them make investments in pollution control equipment that would reduce their emissions.

A market in the credits known as the European Union Emissions Trading Scheme (EU-ETS) has grown up, which allows firms emitting volumes below their allocations to sell their credits to firms exceeding them.

Governments were too generous in the credits allowed under their first National Allocation Plans (2005-07) and polluting firms were able to buy credits at much lower than the penalty rate, so the scheme initially had limited impact. The energy directorate of the European Commission required governments to reduce allocations for their second NAPs (2008-12).[b]

In a further effort to reduce emissions, the Commission obliged members by 2010 to generate 21 percent of all electricity from renewable sources of energy (RES) such as hydro, wind, geothermal and solar - the so-called RES-E objective.[c] Member states were again set variable targets and Greece, despite its highly favourable climate for alternative energies, was assigned a quota below, albeit near, the average. By the end of the decade, it is supposed to be generating 20.1 percent of its power from RES.

The latest available figures (2005) suggested the country was generating around 12 percent. That year's progress report to the Commission from the Ministry of Development posited a best-case scenario that would see the country fall marginally short at 19.8 percent and a worst-case scenario that said it would reach just 14.9 percent.

As of 2005, Greece had some 3,765MW of RES electricity-generating capacity - 3,015MW hydro and 750MW other sources, primarily wind. To achieve the 2010 target, the country needs to add 7,200MW of RES capacity.

In 2006, the government introduced legislation[d] providing priority despatch for RES power producers and offering feed-in tariffs (FITs) for wind, hydro and geothermal units worth approximately 22 percent above then average market prices in order to promote the development of renewables.[e]

The new tariffs attracted intense interest on the part of the Public Power Corporation and major engineering and energy companies who announced tentative plans to install up to 5.3GW of wind farms, investments worth approximately €6.6bn, not counting other RES projects.

The legislation was supposed to speed the licensing process but contained administrative measures that developers say will mean that it will be 2008 before they can acquire production licences (see footnote 10 on page 86). *Moreover, the new subsidiary Land Use Plan governing energy developments had, at the time of writing, not yet come before parliament* (see page 89). *Construction of most of the projects is not expected to start before 2009 at the earliest.*

In April 2007, the European Commission lumped Greece together with four other member states (Cyprus, Ireland, Italy and Latvia) to which it gave formal notice of possible infringement proceedings for having taken "insufficient measures to enable an adequate promotion of renewable energies".

A further scheme[f] to reduce emissions requires member states to ensure that by 2010 all transport fuels contain additives of biofuel equal to 5.75 percent by volume: bioethanol[k] for petrol and biodiesel[h] for gasoil. The Greek government was late in transposing the directive and its legislation[i] contained a fundamental contradiction, which delayed application of a proposed subsidy scheme to promote private development (see footnote 11 on page 86).

State-owned industries such as ELPE and the Hellenic Sugar Industry (EBZ) have since announced plans to develop large-scale production plants.[j]

A directive issued in April 2006[k] called on member states to introduce plans to improve energy efficiency by 9 percent by 2015. The International Energy Agency in its biennial assessment of Greece published in October 2006 concluded that "currently, Greece does not have a comprehensive energy efficiency strategy..." and outlined a 14-point action programme for the government to pursue.[l]

In January 2007, even before Greek government efforts to comply with existing emission targets properly had begun to get off the ground, the European Commission moved on with a new Energy Action Plan,[m] which was endorsed by the spring meeting of the European Council.[n] This committed the EU by 2020 to

- a 20 percent reduction in CO_2 emissions (30 percent if an international agreement to this end can be achieved);
- a 20 percent improvement in energy efficiency; and
- a 10 percent addition of biofuel.

No country limits have yet been set under these new targets but, according to Dr Panagiotis Chaviaropoulos of the Centre for Renewable Energy Sources (KAPE), it could translate into a requirement for Greece to generate 35 percent or more of its electricity from renewable energy sources such as hydro and wind.

[a]Negotiations began in 1997. [b]Greece had a cap of 74.5m t/yr under Phase I (2005-07) but third-party verification of emissions in 2005 showed them to be just 71.3m t/yr. Under Phase II (2008-12) the government and the energy directorate of the commission negotiated a level of 69.1m t/yr. *Wikipedia,* August 10, 2007. [c]Directive 2001/77/EC. [d]Law 3468/06. [e]€73/MWh, compared to a system marginal price in the wholesale market of around €60. For solar generators tariffs stand at €250/MWh up to €450/MWh for small photovoltaic units, a subsidy of between 300 percent and 650 percent. July 18, 2007 the government approved an increase of €2.82/MWh for all RES tariffs; this represented a 3.86 percent increase on the basic €73 rate. [f]Directive 2003/30/EC. [g]Ethanol or methanol distilled from plants with high sugar content such as cane, corn and beet. [h]Esterified seed oils, tallow

or grease (used cooking oils). ʲLaw 3423/05. ʲFor background to the above see Robert McDonald, "Lacklustre Energy", *Business File,* Special Survey No 61, Kerkyra Publications, Athens, October 2006, pp 70-80. ᵏDirective 2006/32/EC. ˡ*Energy policies in IEA countries* - Greece 2006, IEA, Paris, October 2006, p 16. ᵐ"Commission proposes an integrated energy and climate change package to cut emissions for the 21ˢᵗ century", *Press Release,* IP/07/29, Europa, Brussels, January 10, 2007. ⁿ*Presidency Conclusions,* European Council, March 8-9, 2007 (revised), 7224/1/07, Brussels, May 2, 2007.

Privatisation

THE NOTION of privatisation was first promoted by the ND government of Constantine Mitsotakis (1990-93). Its denationalisation efforts provoked confrontation both with the trade union movement, fearful of job losses, and with business interests, concerned about disruption of their sweetheart deals with public enterprises. The proposals were a major factor contributing to that government's downfall.

The resurgent socialists, under the ailing Andreas Papandreou, reversed a large part of ND's progress, but the governments of Costas Simitis accepted that privatisation was a necessary evil if public debt was to be contained at levels that would comply with eurozone convergence targets.

During the period 1998-2003, Pasok governments sold off some €18bn in state assets. The socialists followed the French model, part-privatising firms through listings on the stock exchange, but maintaining a sufficient shareholding to be able to continue to appoint senior management and to control strategic decisions.

The socialists sold off stakes in public utilities (telecoms, electricity, refining and water), infrastructure (ports and highway concessions) and gaming (the football pools and a leading casino).

Five banks were sold outright, though the government retained small stakes in two of the largest commercial banking groups, National and Emporiki.[1]

In opposition, New Democracy, under the leadership of Costas Karamanlis, was critical of Pasok's approach, accusing it of simply selling assets to raise cash. It said that, when elected, its privatisation programme would be designed to promote national development.

The party said that the state had no place in business and implied that it would pursue vigorous denationalisation, promote free markets and reinforce competition through improved regulation.

Its election manifesto suggested, however, that either it had got cold feet or was, at heart, as statist as the socialists. The party platform said that ND would not divest the Public Power Corporation (DEI), the Athens Water and Sewerage Company (EYDAP), the Post Office (ELTA) or Agricultural Bank (ATE) - all of which, it claimed, performed social functions - although it did promise to try to find strategic partners for EYDAP and the Hellenic Telecommunications Organisation (OTE) and to part-float ELTA.

---

[1] For background see Robert McDonald. The Competitiveness of the Greek Economy 2005. pp 95-124.

In office, ND's practices proved similar to those of the socialists, though privatisation sales were conducted at a slower pace. Whereas Pasok sold assets at a rate of about €3bn a year, the rate under ND fell to about €1.8bn a year.

Privatisation remained a divisive issue between the liberal and statist wings of the party and innumerable hours were wasted in the inter-ministerial privatisation committee (IMPC) in inconclusive argument about not only how best to sell assets, but whether they should be sold at all.

By its tally, the ND government raised €6.2bn during the period 2004-07. This, however, is a gross position. In 2004 and again in 2005 there were net negative positions on privatisation transactions in which the government had to pay more to redeem convertible and exchangeable bonds that had been floated by Pasok than was raised through the subsequent sale of the underlying shares. Net privatisation earnings during ND's term were of the order of €5.3bn or €1.5bn a year.

Table 19. Privatisation revenues 2004-07

Company	Date of transaction	Percent sold	Privatisation method	Amount raised by the state (€m)	Currently under state control
Hellenic Petroleum (ELPE)[a]	August 2004	8.21	Trade sale	192	35.49
National Bank of Greece (ETE)	November 2004	7.46	Accelerated bookbuilding	562	0.00
2004				**754**	
Soccer Pools & Lottery Organisation (OPAP)	July 2005	16.44	Secondary offering	1,266	34.00
Hellenic Telecommunications Organisation (OTE)[b]	September 2005	10.00	Accelerated bookbuilding	835	38.70
2005				**2,101**	
Postal Savings Bank (TT)	February 2006	-	Recapitalisation[c]	400	–
Agricultural Bank of Greece (ATE)	May 2006	7.18	Accelerated bookbuilding	328	77.30
Postal Savings Bank (TT)	May 2006	10.00	Sale to Hellenic Post (ELTA)	15 [d]	90.00

Company	Date of transaction	Percent sold	Privatisation method	Amount raised by the state (€m)	Currently under state control
Hellenic Post (ELTA)	May 2006	10.00	Sale to TT	21	90.00
Postal Savings Bank	May 2006	34.84	Initial Public Offering	612	55.16
Emporiki Bank (ET)	August 2006	11.01	Sale to Credit Agricole[e]	364	0.00
2006				**1,740**	
Hellenic Telecommunications Organisation (OTE)	June 2007	10.70	Private placement	1,100	28.00
Postal Savings Bank	July 2007	20.00	Private placement	500	35.16
2007[f]				**1,600**	
Total				**6,195**	

[a]The shares underpinned a convertible bond which fell due in July 2004 and which the Public Portfolio Management Company (DEKA) paid €423m to redeem, ie a net 'loss' on the wider transaction of €331m. [b]The shares formed part of two exchangeable bonds underpinned by 3.05 percent and 10.86 percent of the shares of OTE which the government had redeemed in August 2005 and August 2006 at €530m and €1bn respectively. [c]In 2003, TT paid the Pasok government an extraordinary dividend of €400m, which was booked to budget revenues. The ND government, as part of its 'fiscal housekeeping', ordered the payment reversed, ie this is a book-keeping gain. [d]The listing of TT transformed the worth of this stake to €159m which is payable until 2010. [e]As part of an open market offer. [f]As of mid-July 2007.

Sources: Ministry of Economy and Finance and *Athens News*

Utilities

Prior to 2000, governments were forbidden to sell more than 49 percent of the shares in a public utility. That year, the last Simitis government passed landmark legislation permitting the sale of 50 percent plus.

In every instance, however, governments have maintained a holding of at least a blocking minority third (33.34 percent), thus giving it final say in the appointment of management and strategic decisions.

Hellenic Petroleum (ELPE)

The state stake in the petrochemical company declined to 35.49 percent following the ND government's August 2004 sale of 8.21 percent of the shares to the private Latsis Group. But despite the fact that the 2003 merger between ELPE and Latsis' Petrola refinery includes an implicit agreement that management will pass to the private sector by 2008, the ministry of economy and finance was quick to point out that "no additional rights for the management of the company were given to the existing shareholder".[2]

Since the merger (which took the stake of Petrola's owner, Paneuropean Oil and Industrial Holdings of Luxembourg, to 33.16 percent), the Latsis Group has acquired shares in the open market to take its position to 34.32 percent, also a blocking minority interest.

This has never been exercised, according to ELPA's chief executive Panos Kavoulacos, who says the two main shareholders so far have managed to negotiate all major management decisions without recourse to balloting a general meeting.[3] It remains to be seen whether management will pass to the private sector from 2008 or there will be a further transitional period of joint management.

Hellenic Telecommunications Organisation (OTE)

ND's 2004 manifesto said the government would seek a strategic partner for the company, the implication being that it planned to sell a sufficiently large stake to remove it from public control.

A Pasok government had listed the company in 2000 and through various secondary offerings the state stake was reduced until, at the time of the change of government in 2004, it stood at 35.7 percent.

ND redeemed two bonds that had been issued by the socialists while the stock market was still in decline. The first, a convertible, based on just over 3 percent of the shares, was redeemed in August 2004 at €530m, and the second, an exchangeable, based on 10.7 percent of the shares, matured out of the money in August 2005 and was redeemed at just over €1bn.

This left the state again with a holding close to 49 percent that ND might have offered to a strategic investor, together with the management. At the time, the company was in the red (€292m) because of its voluntary redundancy programme but was well on the way to

---

[2] "Privatisations agenda". Structural reforms. www.mnec.gr.
[3] The ND government appointed as chairman Efthymios Christodoulou, a longstanding party stalwart. However, Kavoulacos, the CEO, is a private sector consultant who was hired from the open market place.

record profits (€509m) in 2006 because of the steep reductions in staff costs.

Instead of a radical course of action, however, the ND government in the autumn of 2005 placed a 10 percent tranche of shares with foreign institutional investors and in late 2006 appointed three merchant banks (one Greek and two Swiss) to find a strategic investor prepared to take a stake of just 20 percent in the share capital and assume a significant voice in the management but without full control.

OTE CEO Panagis Vourloumis said that the ideal strategic investor would be a "big Western European telecommunications company"[4] and, according to press reports, the advisors canvassed Deutsche Telekom, France Telecom and Telefonica of Spain.

In the end, the only expression of interest came from Telecom Austria and in April 2007 it said that it was not interested in making an investment of such magnitude without full management authority.[5]

Ultimately, the government opted for yet another fudge. In June 2007 it placed 10 percent of the shares with foreign institutional investors, raising €1.1bn, and again reducing the state stake to just over a third.[6]

Coincidentally, OTE embarked on a share buy-back scheme which had the effect both of supporting the share price at the time of the private placement and of beginning the process of aggregating sufficient stock for yet another attempt to find a strategic buyer.[7]

ND's approach to OTE has been, at best, ambivalent. Minister of Economy and Finance George Alogoskoufis appeared genuinely to want to divest the company, and Vourloumis certainly was committed to taking it private. But this liberal camp was fought every step of the way by Minister of Transport and Communications Michalis Liapis, an old-style statist, who was determined not to cede public control, and by the company union, OME-OTE, which mounted an elaborate campaign against divestment - including public demonstrations, billboard and media advertising and political lobbying, to which the government

---

[4] "A sale would save OTE", Kathimerini (English edition), December 18, 2006.
[5] "OTE privatization", Greek Equities Daily, EFG Eurobank Securities, April 19, 2007.
[6] 38.7 percent, with approximately 4 percent of that committed to the company pension fund TAP-OTE to compensate for the reduction in contributions caused by the voluntary redundancy programme.
[7] The parent is buying back shares in its listed mobile subsidiary, Cosmote, with a view to boosting turnover to make the company more attractive for sale.

ultimately succumbed in order not to further antagonise the trade union movement ahead of elections.

Public Power Corporation (DEI)

The convoluted procedure adopted for liberalising the electricity and gas sectors effectively precluded privatisation of DEI, although both liberalisation and privatisation could have been achieved simultaneously by following the Italian example (*see page 144*) and simply selling off a bundle of DEI generating assets.[8]

The principal stumbling block was the company union, GENOP-DEI, which adamantly opposed privatisation for fear it would mean cuts in the company's bloated workforce. Labour costs account for about 40 percent of DEI's operating expenses.[9]

The second hurdle was an old-guard middle management, which resisted the notion of unbundling the company's accounts to permit a true picture of the cost of power production.

For example, DEI has preferential access to the country's lignite reserves and the cheap fuel allows it to undercut potential competitors on power price. Unbundling, however, reveals the true cost of carrying on the payroll the 6,000 miners needed to win the brown coal and, when this is coupled with the pollution penalty payments arising from burning the low-calorific-value fuel, the cost weighs heavily on DEI's bottom line.

The 2006 accounts - the first to have been unbundled - showed profits before tax to have slumped to €75.9m compared with €208.7m in 2005 (restated), down from €502.3m in 2004 before unbundling.

In June 2007, the company began to make noises through the press about how it might make sense to sell some 30 percent of its distribution capacity to private suppliers in order to bring the company's retail market share below the 70 percent threshold at which government would cease to fix tariffs.[10]

---

[8] *The OECD, in its 2001 report* Regulatory Reform in Greece, *recommended that DEI sell its two gas-fired generating stations to two different private companies (p 82). Independent market analysts suggest the proposal was impractical since companies need a mix of lignite, hydro and gas plants to be competitive in the wholesale market.*

[9] *Employee numbers have been falling - between 1998 and 2006 they declined from 33,500 to 26,200 - but sales of electricity per employee are still only about two-thirds the level achieved by European peers.*

[10] *"PPC", Investment perspectives, Alpha Finance, June 11, 2007.*

In January 2007, the government appointed a new DEI chairman, Takis Athanasopoulos,[11] who also assumed the title of chief executive officer. Analyst reaction was that the appointment reflected willingness on the part of ND finally to allow market determination of power prices.[12]

Even GENOP was said to be having second thoughts given that, if the company slips into the red, the government could legislate new terms and conditions of employment which could lead to significant staff cuts.[13]

Public Gas Corporation (DEPA)

In its 2007 budget proposal, the government said that it would list DEPA on the Athens Stock Exchange. Press reports spoke of an IPO of around 15 percent of the stock.

In July, however, after the government had approached its target for the year of €1.7bn in privatisation revenues without a DEPA listing, Minister of Economy and Finance George Alogoskoufis said there would be no further sale of utility assets in the course of 2007.

Water

The government did not secure a strategic partner for the Athens Water and Sewerage Company (EYDAP), although the French group Suez, which holds a stake of just under 5 percent in the Thessaloniki Water and Sewage Company (EYATh) made soundings about upping its stake to 25 percent.

Banks

Pasok sold outright a large part of state-controlled banking interests but retained control over two of the main commercial banking groups, National and Emporiki.

In National, the country's largest, it held 7.5 percent direct and voted some 21 percent of the shares held by public pension funds. Shareholdings in the bank were sufficiently widely dispersed that this minority position

---

[11] Former CEO of Toyota Hellas and number two of Toyota Europe.

[12] "...The question is: Could Mr Athanassopoulos do to PPC what Mr Vourloumis did to OTE? We tend to believe the answer is yes but after the elections." Moussos Stathoudakis. PPC. Investment Perspectives. Alpha Finance, January 25, 2007.

[13] "New gov't to decide on PPC's future plans". Kathimerini (English edition). August 18, 2007.

gave the government control, allowing it to appoint senior management.

In Emporiki, the state held 9.4 percent of the shares directly and exercised the vote vested in another 25.5 percent owned by public pension funds, giving it a blocking minority control. From 2000, Crédit Agricole of France built, with government approval, a strategic stake, which stood at 11.13 percent at the time the conservatives took office.

Pasok had started but not completed the process of privatising two former Special Credit Institutions, the Agricultural Bank (ATE) and the Postal Savings Bank (TT).

National Bank of Greece (ETE)

In November 2004, the ND government sold the residual state stake in National Bank through a placement in the London market. It was oversubscribed in a matter of hours and raised €562m.

The government insists that it no longer exercises any influence over National, even though it still controls the votes of the pension fund shares. National's CEO, Takis Arapoglou, also insists there is no government intervention and says that he would resign if there were any interference. Regardless, there is a sense in the market that National remains a state bank.

Emporiki Bank (ET)

Crédit Agricole declared a willingness to increase its stake in Emporiki but only if it could secure a controlling interest. The French suggested that the state should sell not only its direct holding but should persuade pension funds to sell theirs as well.

Alogoskoufis insisted that he could not do this and, after prolonged dickering, finally suggested to Crédit Agricole that it should bundle its holding with that of the state and sell to a third-party strategic investor. The French declined and undertook a series of actions that suggested they might pull out of the bank altogether and leave the government stranded in its search for a partner.

Finally, in June 2006, Crédit Agricole launched an open-market bid for 100 percent of the bank which, after more sparring over price, the government finally accepted, recommending at the same time to the public pension funds that they do likewise. Crédit Agricole acquired 71.9 percent of Emporiki at a price which valued the bank at €3.1bn and garnered €364m for the state.

Agricultural Bank (ATE)

Agricultural Bank was transformed into a universal bank under the Mitsotakis government, although it was still used by the state, under contract, to oversee the farming cooperative movement and to disburse subsidies paid under the EU's Common Agricultural Policy (CAP).

In 2000, Pasok listed 17.6 percent of the bank and shortly before the 2004 election assigned a mandate to Citibank to find a strategic buyer for up to another 49 percent.

In its manifesto, ND said it would not divest the bank but rather would use it to help restructure the extensive debt burden of the Greek farming community.

ATE was one of several Greek banks which effectively breached their capital adequacy ratios following the EU's requirement that listed companies keep their books according to International Financial Reporting Standards. Among other things, IFRS requires that unfunded pension liabilities be subtracted from shareholder value. The ruling bit deeply into Agricultural Bank's asset base.

In May 2005, the government initiated a massive capital injection through a €1.25bn rights issue and in April 2006 it launched a secondary offering of 7.2 percent of ATE's stock on the Athens Exchange. This generated revenues of €328m and reduced the state holding to 77.3 percent.

There have been repeated market rumours that further tranches of 10-25 percent might be offered for sale but the bank's portfolio still needs considerably more restructuring before the shares will command a credible price.

Indeed there is a school of thought that claims the government only sold the small 2006 tranche to avoid the rights issue being investigated by EU competition authorities as illegal state aid, given that the proportion of listed shares is so small and most of those are owned by public pension funds.

Postal Savings Bank (TT)

The socialists had been manoeuvring for some time - and in several different ways - to sell a strategic stake in the Postal Savings Bank (TT). All the major Greek commercial banks had expressed an interest because of the bank's huge deposit base and extensive counter presence in post offices throughout the country. The ND government's preference was for a foreign buyer on the grounds that there already was too much consolidation in the domestic market.

In the event, no foreign buyer proved interested and, in May 2006, the government floated a little over a third of TT's shares (34.84 percent) in an initial public offering on the Athens Exchange raising €612m.

A tranche of 10 percent of the stock of TT was sold to Hellenic Post (ELTA). Ahead of the listing this was valued at €15m; following the listing its value increased to €159m.

The purpose of this manoeuvre was not clear as Hellenic Post remained 100 percent owned by the state. The combined IPO and 'trade sale' reduced the state holding in TT to 55.16 percent.

On July 11, 2007 the government sold a further 10 percent of TT by means of a private placement in Greece and abroad raising €510m and reducing its direct shareholding in the bank to 34.37 percent (44.37% with ELTA's holding).

Attica Bank

The government says that it is ready to sell the state's 35.2 percent indirect stake in the Bank of Attica, which specialises in the financing of public works. The bank is owned 17.2 percent by TT, 15 percent by the Consignments and Loans Fund (a repository of payments owed to the state) and some 41 percent by TSMEDE, the Pension fund of the Engineers and Public Works Contractors.

TSEMEDE would like to take control of the bank but does not have resources to buy a majority stake; it does, however, have a blocking minority stake that allows it to prevent any one else from taking over.

Concessions and PPP

The 'development' aspect of ND's privatisation policy relates to the attraction of private capital for the construction of public infrastructure either through public private partnerships or concession schemes.

The policy had no tangible results during ND's first term, but projects were initiated with an estimated value of more than €10bn.

PPP projects worth approximately €2.5bn were approved for the construction of, among other things, schools, hospitals, courts and local administration offices. A package of motorway concessions worth some €8bn was finally awarded in the first half of 2007, nearly a decade after first having been mooted.

Efforts to develop ports through similar schemes stumbled at the first hurdle (*see page 127-128*) and nothing has come of a promise in the 2007 budget proposal of "market exploitation" of the state's 55 percent stake in Athens International Airport.[14]

As of September 2007, the 12-year licences of eight casinos, authorised as one of the last acts of Pasok under Andreas Papandreou, start to run out. When they were issued they raised the drachma equivalent of €205m.

The Ministry of Economy and Finance has declined to comment on the duration of any extensions that it might offer or how much it might expect to receive for them. A press report has estimated that they might fetch €430m.[15]

The constitution does not permit the state to sell public property outright without parliamentary approval and no effort was made to change this during the process of constitutional reform pursued in 2006-07.

Successive governments have, however, let state properties on long leases and the company managing the venues built for the 2004 Olympics has signed contracts that it claims will generate income of nearly €1.5bn over a horizon of 45 years.

Public-Private Partnerships

Projects undertaken through the Community Support Frameworks involve co-financing, that is they combine public (EU and national) and private funds. The public funds are channelled through the Public Investments Budget.

The ND government has been caught between the Scylla and Charybdis of bringing the budget deficit under control while, at the same time, maximising its uptake of EU structural aid. The simplest way of reducing the deficit - in the light of its unwillingness to reduce the size of the public sector payroll - has been to cut PIB spending. This has meant that the government has had to concentrate all its investment outlays on projects attracting EU aid, leaving in abeyance many nationally-funded projects, which might have been to its political advantage.

Private investment has been limited. With the exception of three large BOT (build-operate-transfer) schemes initiated by the Mitsotakis ND

---

[14] *A plausible scenario mooted at the time was that the government would turn some of the country's larger regional airports into société anonyme (as it has done with the national sea ports) and incorporate part of their assets, together with a portion of those of the DAA, in a real-estate investment trust (REIT) to be listed on the Athens Exchange. At the time of writing, however, nothing had come of the proposal.*
[15] *"Ministers discuss progress of tourism privatizations", Kathimerini (English edition), July 21, 2007.*

government (Attiki Odos, the Athens ring-road; Gefyra, the Rio-Antirio suspension bridge across the mouth of the Gulf of Corinth; and, Athens International Airport at Spata), Greek contractors have been willing to accept contracts for the construction of new infrastructure but not to participate as investors. (The Attiki Odos consortium was led by the Greek construction company, Elliniki Technodomiki, together with J&P Avax, whose parent company is Cypriot, but the Gefyra consortium was led by Vinci of France and the airport consortium by Hochtief of Germany.)

To attract more private investment, the government has promoted the notion of public-private partnerships (PPPs). Under such arrangements private contractors construct public infrastructure, maintain and manage it for a set period of years - usually 20 or more - and recoup their investment cost plus a profit from a pre-defined revenue stream contractually agreed with the public sector.

As with most economic liberalisation policies, Greece came late to the PPP concept. In September 2005, the ND government introduced legislation[16] that instituted standardised rules for relatively small public works valued at under €200m. It is meant to cover projects such as schools, hospitals, waste treatment facilities and provincial ports and airports. The government has excluded the use of PPP contracts for the construction of defence facilities.

The legislation establishes a four-member, Inter-ministerial Committee with three standing ministers - economy, development and Ypehode - plus a fourth having oversight of the sector for which the development is being undertaken (eg, education for schools, health for hospitals etc). The committee is supported by a Special Secretariat housed at the ministry of economy and finance which advises on the viability of projects, facilitates their implementation and provides assistance to public bodies (eg, municipalities) which want to take advantage of such schemes but which may not have the requisite expertise to undertake them.

The legislation stipulates broad rules for financing, fees, permits, environmental protection and expropriation. It also stipulates which agencies can use the format, specifically excluding as private sector participants part-privatised public enterprises such as the Public Power Corporation.

Once approved by the Special Secretariat, the contractual fee is

[16] Law 3389/05.

incorporated in the Public Investment Budget. If the private developer does not fulfil the conditions of the contract, there are provisions for it to be revoked.

PPPs were pioneered in the UK under New Labour and at first seemed a panacea for the development of public infrastructure without the need for public borrowing. As the process has begun to mature, however, it has been seen to have considerable problems as original developers have sold on their stakes to secondary interests with, in some instances, a severe decline in standards of maintenance and service.

Conversely, public agencies have attached such rigorous conditions to other projects that the private contractors have not been able to profit from their deals.[17]

At the time of writing, the Special Secretariat had approved projects with indicative budgets totalling €2.5bn including, among other things, 81 schools, six university buildings, three hospitals, three prisons, five local authority buildings, two courts and seven fire stations.

In a few cases, tenders for technical, legal and financial advisors had been completed or were close to completion but in none had the PPP tenders for works and operations got underway, yet alone been completed. At the rate the tendering process was progressing it looked as if it would be the third quarter of 2008 before any of the projects might be assigned, let alone begin to be constructed.

Meanwhile, costs have been mounting. A list of approved projects published during the first half of 2007 gave indicative budgets on average 20 percent higher than a similar list published during the latter half of 2006.

Table 20. Projects approved by the Special Secretariat for Public-Private Partnerships[a]

Sector & contracting authority	Contract	Duration (years)	Project	Budget (€m)[b]	Status	Closing date
Ministry of Education & Religious Affairs						
Organisation of School Buildings (OSK)	Financing, construction, facility management	25	23 school buildings: Eastern and Western Macedonia, Thrace, Epirus, Ionian Islands	76	Tender for technical, legal & financial advisors; PPP tender	26.07.07 Q1.08

[17] In mid-July 2007. Metronet Alliance, a consortium that had won the contract to maintain a number of the major lines of London Underground Limited went into administration because it found the requirements of its contract more costly than anticipated.

Sector & contracting authority	Contract	Duration (years)	Project	Budget (€m)[b]	Status	Closing date
Ministry of Education & Religious Affairs						
OSK	Financing, construction, facility management	25	31 school buildings: Macedonia	140	Tender for technical, legal and financial advisors; PPP tender	09.07 Q4.08
OSK	Financing, construction, facility management	25	27 school buildings: Attica	180	OSK evaluating bids for advisors; PPP tender	06.07 Q4.07
OSK	Financing, construction, facility management	25	6 buildings, University of the Peloponnese: Tripoli, Kalamata, Corinth, Nafplio, Sparta	100	Preparation of tender documents for SPV to undertake projects; PPP tender	n.d. Q4.07
Ministry of Health & Social Solidarity						
Public Hospitals Construction Organisation (Depanom)	Financing, construction, maintenance, facility	27	Paediatric Hospital, Thessaloniki	389	Depanom evaluating bids for advisors	n.d.
Depanom	Financing, construction, maintenance, facility management	27	Oncological Hospital, Thessaloniki	396	Depanom evaluating bids for adivsors	n.d.
Depanom	Financing, construction, maintenance, facility management	27	General Hospital, Preveza	131	Tender for technical, legal & financial advisors	12.09.07
Ministry of Internal Affairs, Public Management & Decentralisation						
Region of Epirus	Reconstruction Domboli Building Complex, Ioannina	25	Accommodation for Regional Services	16[c]	Tender for technical, legal & financial advisors	06.07
Prefecture of Corinth	Financing, construction, maintenance, facility management	25	Government House for Prefecture, Corinth	19[c]	Tender for technical, legal & financial advisors	18.06.07
Prefecture of Trikala	Financing, construction, maintenance, facility management	25	Government House for Prefecture, Trikala	19[c]	Tender for technical, legal & financial advisors	18.06.07
Prefecture of Achaia	Financing, construction, maintenance, facility management		Government House for Prefecture, Patra	30[c]	Tender for technical, legal & financial advisors	04.09.07
Prefecture of Fthiotida	Financing, construction, maintenance, facility management		Government House for Prefecture, Lamia	28[c]	Tender for technical, legal & financial advisors	04.09.07

Sector & contracting authority	Contract	Duration (years)	Project	Budget (€m)[b]	Status	Closing date
Ministry of Public Order						
Hellenic Public Real Estate Company (KED)	Financing, construction, maintenance, facility management	25	11 buildings for Hellenic Police (ELAS)	149	PPP tender	Q4.07
Hellenic Police Force/KED	Facility management; energy efficiency improvements	15	4 buildings of ELAS	36	PPP tender	Q4.07
Hellenic Fire Brigade/KED	Financing, construction, maintenance, facility management	24	7 fire stations	38	Tender for private contractor; contract award	06.07 Q1.08
Ministry of Justice						
Themis Kataskevastiki	Financing, construction, maintenance, facility management	25	3 prisons: Thessaloniki, Volos, Corinth	238	Themis evaluating bids for advisors; PPP tender	09.07 Q1.08
Themis Kataskevastiki	Financing, construction, maintenance, facility	25	2 Courts of Justice: Patra, Iraklio	120	Tender for legal, technical & financial advisors launched	06.07
Ministry of Culture						
General Secretariat for Olympic Utilisation	Transformation Tae Kwon Do Stadium; financing, construction, maintenance, facility management	25	International Conference Centre for Athens, Faliro	65	PPP tender	07.07
Ministry of Merchant Marine						
Local port authorities	Installation & operation	8	Security systems, 12 ports: Alexandroupolis, Corfu, Elefsina, Iraklio, Igoumenitsa, Kavala, Lavrio, Patra, Piraeus, Rafina, Thessaloniki, Volos	342	Tender for technical, legal & financial advisors	31.07.07
Total				2,512[d]		

[a] *Under Law 3389/2005.* [b] *In each instance the budget is supplemented by the costs of heavy maintenance and 20 percent of the insurance.* [c] *Figures taken from an undated document posted on the Special Secretariat website; another document from the site, also undated, but, from internal evidence having been posted later, aggregates the five administrative buildings at a total cost of €135.5m. Interestingly, the estimated cost of all the projects increases significantly - by 20 percent and more - between publication of the two documents.* [d] *€2,535.5 with the aggregated figure referred to in footnote "c" above.*

Source: Special Secretariat for Public-Private Partnerships, www.ppp.mnec.gr

Highway concessions

In 1998, the Simitis government incorporated in CSF III six major highway schemes to be built as concession projects. They were to be a combination of new highways, repairs to old, and longterm maintenance contracts to be paid for through real[18] and shadow tolling[19]. At the time the projects were estimated to cost some €3.8bn.

A tendering process was initiated in January 2001 which was supposed to have been adjudicated by mid-2003. It attracted the interest of 19 consortia and joint ventures consisting of 58 construction companies of which 25 were foreign.

Greek contractors - overstretched with projects ahead of the Olympic Games - asked that the tendering process be delayed so that they would not lose the business to the foreigners. Later in 2001, the Pasok government introduced legislation revamping the classification system for public contractors,[20] leading to a wave of mergers and acquisitions in the industry. This changed the composition of some of the original bidding consortia. Alliances had to be reformed and the original bids recast.

By late 2003, however, the process was completed and a special service at the Ministry of Environment, Town Planning and Public Works (Ypehode) was seeking to move the tender forward.[21]

When the government changed, the tendering process was up and running and all the incoming New Democracy government had to do was pick up where the socialists had left off. This would have given a major fillip to the construction industry, which in 2005 suffered a slump so severe that several large contractors went bankrupt.

The new minister, George Souflias, regardless, took over a year to review the process. Bids were not reconsidered until 2006 and most contracts not awarded until mid-2007. At the time of writing, some of the contracts had yet to be approved by parliament.

It will be 2008 at least before most of the projects get off the ground and target dates (as early as 2009) for completion of some of the projects

---

[18] *Under new arrangements, tolls will be charged by distance travelled and not per entry into the system.*
[19] *Fees pre-agreed according to traffic estimates rather than actual use.*
[20] *Law 2940/01. For background see Robert McDonald, "Heavy stuff", Special Survey No 48, Business File, Kerkyra Publications, Athens, June 2003, p 21.*
[21] *Special Service of Public Works, Concession of Roads (EYDE-OAP). There would appear to have been a power struggle going on between ministries as the legislation governing the projects called for the central coordinating authority to be the Ministry of Economy and Finance.*

will almost certainly slip by a year, if not more. Meanwhile, the estimated cost of the projects has more than doubled to stand at over €8bn.

Table 21. Toll-road concessions

Consortium	Project	Length (km)	Estimated cost (€bn)	Completion date
Aegean Motorway Concession[a]	Maliakos-Kleidi	231	1.15	2010
Apion Kleos[b]	Elefsina-Patra & Pyrgos-Tsakona	365	2.70[c]	2014
Moreas SA[d]	Corinth-Tripoli-Kalamata & Lefktro-Sparta	205	1.04	2009
Hellenic Autopistas[e]	Rio-Antirio - Ioannina (Ionian Highway)	382	1.39	2010
Hellenic Autopistas	Lamia-Grevena (Central Greece Motorway, E65)	232	0.53	2012
Elliniki Technodomiki[f]	Thessaloniki Submarine Bypass	4	0.47	n/a
Pending	Attiki Odos Extension[g]	36	0.90	n/a
Total			**8.18**	

[a]*Hochtief PPP Solutions GmbH, Germany (35 percent); Elliniki Technodomiki TEV (20 percent); J&P Avax (16.25 percent); Vinci, France (13.75 percent); Aegek (10 percent); Athena (5 percent). J&P is in the process of taking over Athena and at the time of writing controlled 71 percent.* [b]*Vinci, France (36 percent); Hochtief Projektentwicklung, Germany (25 percent); Elliniki Technodomiki TEV (18 percent); J&P-Avax (18 percent); Athena (3 percent).* [c]*Of which €550m is to be put up by the state.* [d]*Elliniki Technodomiki TEV (73.34 percent); Pantechniki SA (13.33 percent); Intrakat/Intracom Holdings (13.33 percent). ELTEV has acquired Pantechniki.* [e]*Cintra/Dragados, Spain (66.67 percent); GEK/Terna (33.33 percent).* [f]*50 percent.* [g]*Three extensions of the Ymittos peripheral road (part of the Attiki Odos system) to Rafina on the Aegean coast and to Vouliagmeni and to Elliniko on the Saronic coast.*

Sources: *Athens News; Kathimerini (English edition)***; Athens Exchange;** *Greek Equities Daily,* **EFG Eurobank Securities; and,** *Greek Equities Daily Watch,* **Alpha Finance**

Public property development

The Greek state has a vast property portfolio, which successive governments have tried to develop, in virtually every instance through leasing the assets rather than selling them outright.

The Hellenic Real Estate Development Corporation (KED), an adjunct of the ministry of economy and finance (YpOi), manages an estimated 100,000 state properties comprising some 20,000 square kilometres, or 15 percent of the Greek landmass.

In 2000, Pasok created Hellenic Tourist Properties (ETA) to manage and develop the assets of the National Tourism Organisation (EOT). Title to the properties is still held by EOT, which reports to the Ministry of Tourism but the development rights have been transferred to ETA, which also is an adjunct of YpOi.

In 2003, the last Pasok government created Hellenic Olympic Properties (OA) to manage 12 of the 18 Olympic venues that were constructed by the state (Ypehode and the ministry of culture through the Secretariat for Sport) at a budgetary cost of some €1.7bn. Plans called for two of the sites to be sold to ETA. Under ND the company was restructured and given the responsibility for managing all 18 sites.

Hellenic Tourist Properties (ETA)
and the Tourism Development Company (ETA)

Hellenic Tourist Properties devised a development format wherein it created, together with private contractors, special-purpose vehicles (SPVs) to which it contributed its development rights, while the contractors provided development and operating capital.

The private interests were awarded longterm leases against initial cash payments and annual fees, the latter usually based on a percentage of turnover. Using this formula (or variations on it), ETA had 'privatised' by 2004 five Attica beaches, three marinas, two large Xenia hotels and the Mont Parnes casino.

At the time of the government change, ETA had announced (or was already embarked upon) tenders for further such joint ventures involving refurbishment of the Corfu casino, the creation of a convention centre in the east terminal of the old Athens airport, renovation and expansion of the Afantou golf course on Rhodes and the construction of a theme park in the Anavyssos Alikes estate on the east coast of Attica, some 50km south of Athens.

Pasok announced its intention to list ETA on the Athens Exchange and, to this end, sold €800m in *prometocha* - bonds that were to be exchangeable into shares at a discount during the IPO. (At the time of writing, a written query to the management as to what had become of them had not been answered.)

The ND government suspended the Pasok programme, recast the agency as the Tourism Development Company (also, confusingly, having the acronym ETA) and announced that it would continue a development programme but without state participation.

The new ETA published several pre-prospectuses proposing to develop Faliro Marina, the Afantou golf course, the Corfu casino, Anavyssos and a clutch of Xenia hotels,[22] but none of the proposals made it through the inter-ministerial privatisation committee where there was intense wrangling between the Ministries of Tourism and Economy and Finance over disposition of proceeds, given the division of ownership and management rights. Two managing directors of ETA resigned and the rationale for the existence of the company was called into question. It was summer 2007 before a third managing director, Harry Coccossis, a highly efficient former special advisor to the Ministry of Tourism,[23] finally succeeded in getting clearance for the sales.

In August, when it was apparent that elections were imminent, ETA began to advertise[24] for an outright buyer for the Corfu casino and for longterm leaseholders (60 years) for Afantou and the Anavyssos estate. Expressions of interest were due by end-October.

Hellenic Olympic Properties (OA)

Development of the Olympic property portfolio benefited from the fact that prime minister personally held the post of minister of culture, which was responsible for the Secretariat of Sport, the state body with responsibility for the Olympic Games.[25] Under his auspices, legislation[26]

---

[22] *The convention centre at Elliniko was challenged in the courts by families whose properties had been expropriated for the airport claiming that if the land was to revert to private ownership it should revert to them.*

[23] *His predecessor had been a protégé of the Minister of Economy and Finance.*

[24] Financial Times, *August 8, 2007 and* International Herald Tribune, *August 9, 2007.*

[25] *Athens 2004, which actually ran the Games, was a public company but primarily funded from resources provided through the aegis of the International Olympic Committee.*

[26] *Law 3342/05.*

governing disposal of the properties was rushed through parliament within nine months of the conclusion of the Games - a record time in Greece for a subject of such complexity and inter-ministry responsibility.[27]

Hellenic Olympic Properties (OA) appears to have been efficient about finding developers to take properties off its hands but is highly uncommunicative about details of the contracts it has signed and their terms of reference.

OA claims that it has done deals with a total worth of nearly €1.5bn over a period of 45 years, when lessees' initial payments and annual fees are aggregated.

Table 22. Use of Olympic venues

Site	Venue	Contractor	New use	Award	Price (€m) Investment Annual fees	Concession (years)
Faliro	Indoor arena for Tae Kwon Do	PPP development; under tender	Metropolitan convention centre	Four consortia shortlisted January 2007	94 n/a	25
Elliniko	Agios Kosmas Marina	Seirios (consortium) led by the construction company, Attikat	Marina plus hotel and retail	Preliminary offers under evaluation (April 2007)	n/a 14.5/yr	45
Maroussi	International Broadcast Centre	Lamda Development	Shopping mall	August 2006	60 7.25/yr (revised upwards in years 2-15 by the CPI + 2% to a maximum of 9.6; thereafter by the CPI)	40

Site	Venue	Contractor	New use	Award	Price (€m) Investment Annual fees	Concession (years)
Goudi	Badminton Hall	Adam, Georgas and Kontoyiannis	Theatre, 2,500 seats	n/d	6 n/a	20
Galatsi	Indoor Stadium	Acropole-Charagionis/ Sonae Sierra	Shopping mall	June 2007	78 3/yr (rising to 4)	40
Elliniko	Canoe-Kayak Slalom	J&P Avax-GEK-Vioter-Corfu Water Park	Water park	January 2007	4.6 n/a	30
Faliro	Beach Volleyball		Theatre & concert venue	April 2006 expressions of interest[a]	n/a n/a	15

[a]*There were three Greek bidders (Village Roadshow Operations; a consortium led by the fast-food company Everest; and another led by the contractors' GEK) plus two from France. At the time of writing there was no indication on the company website of how the tender was adjudicated.*

Sources: Press reports, company annual reports, www.olympicproperties.gr

Hellenic Real Estate Development Corporation (KED)

Pasok was working on packaging a number of prime properties from the KED portfolio as a real-estate investment trust (REIT) to be floated on the Athens Exchange.

The socialists' scheme was cancelled by the ND administration of YpOi. It was implied that it would pursue the concept but that the underlying assets in the REIT needed to be considerably increased in value, in order to increase earnings to support the share price. The idea was quietly allowed to drop.

Instead, KED has drawn up a business plan to 2013 which foresees it developing a total of 205 of the properties in its portfolio. It has eight under contract (€95m), three under tender (€33m) and 194 under development (€2.2bn).

It also has large tracts of land on Corfu, Rhodes and in the Peloponnese which it is considering tendering for real-estate development under 50-year concession agreements. As of June 2007 it was searching for an investment advisor (either a bank or a developer) to give it guidance as to how best to proceed.

Many of the properties that are being developed under PPP arrangements have come from the KED bank of managed properties.

'Implementation deficit'

COMPETITIVENESS arises from an amalgam of factors: a stable economic climate to promote growth, administrative reform to facilitate entrepreneurship and liberalised markets to promote competition.

The New Democracy government performed well on the macroeconomic and fiscal fronts but, while it introduced extensive administrative reforms in law, it made little headway in their practical implementation.

Its record on liberalisation could at best be described as disappointing. It went through the motions of passing legislation to liberalise network industries in order to comply with EU directives but failed to put in place operating codes and other practices with the result that markets will not be open before the end of the decade - if then.

On the macroeconomic front, the government updated the calculation of gross domestic product by 25 percent, which, assuming the methodology is validated by Eurostat, will bring the nominal standard of living significantly closer to the EU median - something that is already observable from the Greek lifestyle, at least in urban centres.

The conservative administration, controversially, carried out a programme of fiscal housekeeping which re-allocated budget deficits and aggregate debt in a manner more compliant with the convergence criteria of the Economic and Monetary Union which underpin the common currency, the euro.

It was largely a paper exercise - on a cash basis the government continued to struggle to make budgetary ends meet - but it brought Greek practice more closely into line with the practices of eurozone partners and won the approbation of the European Commission, the arbiter of the rules.

The ND government committed to pursuing a balanced budget by 2010 and to growth policies designed to bring the Greek standard of living to a par with that in the eurozone sometime during the following decade.

The government did not, however, tackle the crucial issue of pension reform. The Greek system has unfunded liabilities in excess of 200 percent of GDP and annually absorbs public expenditure equivalent to approximately 12.5 percent of GDP.

According to the OECD,[1] that will double by 2050 unless there are fundamental changes to the system. The problem is that the contributors

---

[1] *For a full discussion of the issue see* Greece, *Vol 207/5, OECD, Paris, May 2007, pp 67-84.*

- employees, employers and the government - cannot agree the best mode of correction: improved administration, amalgamation of the multitudinous funds, higher contributions, lower pensions, later retirement age etc.

While the pensions issue does not have a direct bearing on external competitiveness, it has significant ramifications for the domestic economy, particularly on future GDP growth.

The ND government was not particularly successful in drawing aid for investment in infrastructure and other development programmes from EU structural funds under the Third Community Support Framework (2000-06).

It inherited from the Pasok government funds allocation and disbursement procedures of which the European Commission disapproved and it failed to rectify them in a timely manner so that in 2005 it was forced to rebate €500m that already had been spent.

Failure thereafter to keep to timetables meant that in 2006 it was forced to reschedule a number of programmes so that €1.2bn in co-financing from Brussels under CSF III was put at risk and another €1bn probably lost to the National Strategic Reference Framework (2007-13).

With about 15 percent of the allotted time remaining in which to absorb the aid funds on offer from Brussels under CSF III, the government had approximately 40 percent of the money still to spend and was unlikely to be able to do so in a manner acceptable to the commission under new accounting procedures.

Although the government would never admit to this, it gave the impression during 2006 of having set to one side the programmes of CSF III (many of which were unlikely to be finished on time and not of its making in the first place) to concentrate on the formulation of projects of its own design for the forthcoming ESPA.

These shift the focus from spending on 'hard' infrastructure to 'soft' actions that promote education and training, digitalisation and administrative reform designed to comply with the EU's current emphasis on skills and job creation under the Lisbon Strategy. While the concepts have been canvassed and catalogued, most programmes remain at the study or development stage.

In 2007, the first year of the ESPA, the government was already falling behind in disbursement of the €20.4bn in Brussels funding aid available under the National Strategic Reference Framework.

The ND administration introduced headline policies to promote investment, including a reduction in the rate of corporation tax by 10 percentage points to 25 percent and subsidies for small and medium enterprises prepared to establish in the regions. Their impact has yet to be fully assessed but the initial results were viewed positively.

It had less success with venture capital programmes, inherited from Pasok, that were designed to promote cutting-edge business in new technologies; its own proposed VC fund to promote ICT failed to get off the ground.

The government also went through the motions of administrative reform designed to cut red tape and to make the bureaucracy more responsive. By its own admission, though, the results were notional rather than practical. The reforms reshaped the Civil Service Code, changed job descriptions and set new guidelines for productivity, but changes in practices were scarce.

Similarly, the government passed a wide-ranging law to streamline the operation of public enterprises and entities (DEKOs), designed to make them adhere to corporate principles and at least consider the concept of profit. The legislation ran headlong into the inertia of this heavily overstaffed, frequently vestigial, segment of the public sector and deadlines for change kept having to be pushed back. At best the legislation could be said to have made the DEKOs justify the annual subsidies that they require to sustain their existence.

An effort was made, with some success, to reduce red tape in registering and permitting businesses but clearing title on a property or getting planning permission remained a major hurdle because there is as yet no Land Registry or National Land Use Plan. Both of these are the responsibility of the Ministry of Environment, Town Planning and Public Works (Ypehode), which continued its historical tradition of allowing political concerns to supersede technical considerations in the elaboration of policy.

Changes were made to improve the antiquated Companies Act and to the bankruptcy law in order to make it possible to try to salvage a business in financial trouble. Little or no progress was made, though, in breaking closed shops (particularly in the professions) or curbing cartels (particularly in markets for domestically manufactured products).

The ND government trod softly so far as the trade union movement was concerned. It did do away with punitive overtime rates that had been designed to force employers into hiring more workers and focussed instead on creating schemes for the young, the longterm unemployed and for women. It promoted the notion of training, retraining and lifelong learning but, again, most of the programmes are still at the stage of planning and design.

The government did create a unified pension fund for bank workers but primarily to facilitate its efforts at privatisation in the sector. It backed the management of the Hellenic Telecommunications Organisation (OTE) in its massive redundancy programme in hopes of creating new terms of reference for employment in public enterprises that would make their privatisation easier in the future. Typically, the government used a combination of stick and carrot, coupling legislation that changed terms of employment with promises of a hefty subsidy of the workers' pension fund.

The effort to reform tertiary education came badly unstuck. An evaluation system for universities and their staff was introduced but represented the lowest common denominator of all the interests involved. Modest independent proposals for teaching and administrative reforms that would have linked the provision of funding to the results of evaluation, were heavily watered down in the course of yearlong consultations that also provided the focus for repeated, sometimes violent, protest actions by recalcitrant academics and students.

Poor political leadership meant that the government failed properly to distinguish for the public the concept of reform of current practice from a parallel proposal to amend the Constitution to allow the functioning of not-for-profit private universities. The aspiration had been to establish an alternative tertiary hierarchy that would provide benchmarking for, and competition with, the state system in hopes of promoting the latter's improvement. The upshot was that the government squandered a huge repository of political capital to little effect.

The ND party in opposition presented itself as the party of the free market. It said that the state had no role in business but should rather ensure sound and even-handed market regulation.

In office, it proved itself to be nearly as statist as its socialist predecessors. It has retained control over all major public utilities and, while it has gone through the motions of compliance with EU directives on liberalisation, it has in practice repeatedly put obstacles in the way of market opening.

The exception is telecoms, where the regulator has been given autonomy and the market has been fully opened with the result that in the past five years there have been foreign capital inflows into the country of the order of €7bn.

In other sectors, there is talk of investment in projects worth some €28.5bn:

- €8bn in highway concessions, €6bn in ports and €2.5bn in public-private partnership schemes;

- €6.6bn in RES projects, €2bn in thermal energy generating stations, and €1.8bn in the northern gas pipeline; and

- at least €1.5bn in pending leisure-integrated developments with perhaps more to come through the exploitation of tourist and Olympics' properties.

But it remains talk either because of delays in introducing the necessary enabling legislation or in implementing laws already in place.

Stefanos Manos, the maverick ex-ND minister of economy and finance who was elected to the last parliament on the Pasok ticket but sat as an independent, always used to criticise Pasok saying that its greatest failing was that it "failed to take into account the cost of delay". The socialists suffered from a θα syndrome, ie they were always about to do something in the future.

New Democracy, by contrast, has made extensive programme commitments and churned out massive - some might say excessive - amounts of legislation. The problem is its lack of application.

The OECD in its 2007 report on the Greek economy spoke of what it termed an "implementation deficit" in which it said "worthy legislation is not implemented in timely fashion".[2]

August 20, 2007

---

[2] Greece. *Volume 2007/5. OECD. Paris. May 2007. p 92.*

Annex

*1. Results of recent national elections

Party	2000		2004		2007	
	% of votes	No. of seats	% of votes	No. of seats	% of votes	No. of seats
New Democracy (ND)	42.7	125	45.4	165	41.9	152
Panhellenic Socialist Movement (Pasok)	43.8	158	40.6	117	38.1	102
Greek Communist Party (KKE)	5.5	11	5.9	12	8.2	22
Coalition of the Radical Left (SyRizA)	3.2	6	3.3	6	5.0	14
Popular Orthodox Rally (Laos)	–	–	2.2	–	3.8	10
Others	4.8	–	2.6	–	3.0	–
Total	100.0	300	100.0	300	100.0	300

Source: Ministry of the Interior

*2. On October 8 Eurostat validated an uplift of 9.6 percent bringing estimated 2007 GDP to €229.4bn.

*3. On November 6, the financial news agency *Bloomberg* reported that the government would introduce legislation requiring firms to pay any unpaid tax in four equal installments to March 2008.

*4. According to a report, citing "government sources" *in Kathimerini (English edition)*, October 8, the Ministry of the Internal Affairs, Public Administration and Decentralisation is working on legislation to reduce: regions from 13 to six; prefectures from 52 to 16; and, municipalities from 1,034 to 400. The mayor of Athens Nikitis Kaklamanis, who is also president of the Central Union of Municipalities (KEDKE), called at KEDKE's annual conference in November for abolition altogether of the prefectural level of the administration and the merger of its elected councils into the regional level of government or into Metropolitan Authorities for large conurbations such as Athens and Thessaloniki.

*5. On December 3, the Competition Committee handed down fines totalling €47.7m on the country's five largest dairy companies – Vivartia (€16m), Mevgal (€13.17m), Fage (€9.13m), Nestle (€6.18m) and Olymbos (€3.19m) . The companies were accused of having colluded to form a cartel that would ensure uniformly high milk prices in supermarkets and low prices to dairy producers. The Association of Greek Milk Industries (AGMI) was said to have been aware of the price-fixing arrangements and was threatened with a €5m fine if the practices were not ended immediately. See "Dairy companies fined 48m euros for price fixing," *Athens News,* December 7, 2007.

*6. As of November 20, the state had still not transferred the shares to the pension fund. (See also *9.)

*7. The 2008 budget published on November 20 included €1.1 bn (0.5 percent of GDP) for settlement of debts to Olympic and relief for the victims of the August forest fires but did not break down how much for which.

*8. Intracom reportedly had planned to merge HOL, Teledome and Unibrain, another ICT company, into a telecom operator that would be listed. November 28, 2007 *Greek Equities Daily,* the electronic brokerage newsletter of Eurobank Securities reported that, after doing due diligence Intracom, decided not to proceed with the acquisition of Teledome.

*9. Marfin Investment Group (MIG), a private equity company associated with Marfin Popular Bank and backed by the Dubai Financial Group, had acquired (as of December 6, 2007) 18.46% of the Hellenic Telecommunications Organisation (OTE) through open market operations. As the second largest shareholder after the state (28%), it demanded seats on the board. MIG was believed to be acting as the cats paw for the Emirates telecommunications company, Etisalat. The government said, that while it seeks a strategic investor, it wants one from a European Union member state and made it clear it would seek to frustrate any hostile takeover bid. December 7, the Ministry of Economy and Finance submitted an amendment to Parliament limiting to 20% the stake that investors can hold in companies of strategic importance unless there is special dispensation given by an inter-ministerial privatisation committee. The government claimed to have the approval of the European Commission for the measure. See "Grip kept on state firms, *Kathimerini (English edition),* December 8-9, 2007.

*10. In September the cap was lifted completely.

*11. The government has re-committed to establishing a formula to reimburse DEI under PSOs but as of the beginning of December 2007 had not yet produced one. In October, the new chief executive officer of DEI, Panayotis Athanassopoulos, published a draft business plan which, called for the creation of six subsidiary companies (mining, transport, generation, transmission, distribution and sales) which were supposed to trade amongst themselves on commercial principles. The draft outlined an investment programme, which would have seen a fuel shift for thermal generating plants away from polluting domestic lignite to cleaner-burning imported hard coal and natural gas and could possibly have led to lay-offs among the 6,000 workers in the mining division. Militants from the company union occupied Athanassopoulos' office and called upon the government to sack him. The ND government, with its slim majority and fearful of power strikes in the winter months, persuaded the DEI management to conduct six months of talks with the union about the desirability/feasibility of the proposals (reminiscent of what happened when OLP tried to redevelop its container terminal, *see page 127).* When the final version of the business plan was published in late November, the DEI management said it still thought the creation of the subsidiaries the 'optimal' structure for the company. It called for an unbundling of end user tariffs (plus an oil price adjuster) to help it finance an €11.2bn investment programme to 2014 including €4bn worth of new thermal generating plant (800MW of gas-fired plant, 1,600MW of hard coal plant and 900MW of modern lignite-burning plant); €2bn in renewable energy projects (RES); and, €5.2bn in improvements to the transmission and distribution systems that would permit the connection of the RES plants (with their erratic power production) to the grid. To see it through current financial difficulties (DEI posted a loss in the third quarter of 2007), the company requested an immediate average increase in tariffs of 21.7%. November 30, the Development Minister, Christos Folias, announced a complex schedule of increases in low, medium and high voltage tariffs to be phased in between December 1, 2007 and July 1, 2008 which would produce an uplift that market analysts have calculated will average 11%. From January 1, 2009 a formula to allow adjustments in fuel prices would apply for fuel oil and natural gas.

Index